PROPANE FOR
CHEC

Company Name: _____

Date Used: _____

Notes / Remarks

_____
_____
_____
_____
_____
_____
_____
_____
_____
_____
_____
_____
_____

PROPANE FORKLIFT INSPECTION CHECKLIST

Date: _____ Shift: _____

Forklift Serial Number: _____

Hour Meter Start: _____ End: _____ Total Hours: _____

	Gas gauge		Hour Meter
	LPG tank and locator pin		Hydraulic Controls
	LPG tank hose		Lights - Head and Tail
	Accelerator		Lights - Warning
	Alarms		Mast
	Battery Connector		Oil Leaks
	Belt		Oil Pressure
	Brakes - Parking		Overhead Guard
	Engine Oil Level		Radiator Level
	Forks		Safety Equipment
	Fuel		Steering
	Gauges		Tires
	Horn		Unusual Noises
	Hoses		Other: _____

Notes: _____
_____
_____
_____
_____
_____

Operator's Name	Supervisor's Name
_____	_____
Operator's Signature	Supervisor's Signature
_____	_____

PROPANE FORKLIFT INSPECTION CHECKLIST

Date: _____ Shift: _____

Forklift Serial Number: _____

Hour Meter Start: _____ End: _____ Total Hours: _____

	Gas gauge		Hour Meter
	LPG tank and locator pin		Hydraulic Controls
	LPG tank hose		Lights - Head and Tail
	Accelerator		Lights - Warning
	Alarms		Mast
	Battery Connector		Oil Leaks
	Belt		Oil Pressure
	Brakes - Parking		Overhead Guard
	Engine Oil Level		Radiator Level
	Forks		Safety Equipment
	Fuel		Steering
	Gauges		Tires
	Horn		Unusual Noises
	Hoses		Other: _____

Notes: _____
_____
_____
_____
_____
_____
_____

Operator's Name	Supervisor's Name
_____	_____
Operator's Signature	Supervisor's Signature
_____	_____

PROPANE FORKLIFT INSPECTION CHECKLIST

Date: _____ Shift: _____

Forklift Serial Number: _____

Hour Meter Start: _____ End: _____ Total Hours: _____

	Gas gauge		Hour Meter
	LPG tank and locator pin		Hydraulic Controls
	LPG tank hose		Lights - Head and Tail
	Accelerator		Lights - Warning
	Alarms		Mast
	Battery Connector		Oil Leaks
	Belt		Oil Pressure
	Brakes - Parking		Overhead Guard
	Engine Oil Level		Radiator Level
	Forks		Safety Equipment
	Fuel		Steering
	Gauges		Tires
	Horn		Unusual Noises
	Hoses		Other: _____

Notes: _____
_____
_____
_____
_____
_____

Operator's Name

_____

Operator's Signature

_____

Supervisor's Name

_____

Supervisor's Signature

_____

PROPANE FORKLIFT INSPECTION CHECKLIST

Date: _____ Shift: _____

Forklift Serial Number: _____

Hour Meter Start: _____ End: _____ Total Hours: _____

	Gas gauge		Hour Meter
	LPG tank and locator pin		Hydraulic Controls
	LPG tank hose		Lights - Head and Tail
	Accelerator		Lights - Warning
	Alarms		Mast
	Battery Connector		Oil Leaks
	Belt		Oil Pressure
	Brakes - Parking		Overhead Guard
	Engine Oil Level		Radiator Level
	Forks		Safety Equipment
	Fuel		Steering
	Gauges		Tires
	Horn		Unusual Noises
	Hoses		Other: _____

Notes: _____
_____
_____
_____
_____
_____

Operator's Name	Supervisor's Name
Operator's Signature	Supervisor's Signature

PROPANE FORKLIFT INSPECTION CHECKLIST

Date: _____ Shift: _____

Forklift Serial Number: _____

Hour Meter Start: _____ End: _____ Total Hours: _____

	Gas gauge		Hour Meter
	LPG tank and locator pin		Hydraulic Controls
	LPG tank hose		Lights - Head and Tail
	Accelerator		Lights - Warning
	Alarms		Mast
	Battery Connector		Oil Leaks
	Belt		Oil Pressure
	Brakes - Parking		Overhead Guard
	Engine Oil Level		Radiator Level
	Forks		Safety Equipment
	Fuel		Steering
	Gauges		Tires
	Horn		Unusual Noises
	Hoses		Other: _____

Notes: _____

_____

_____

_____

_____

_____

Operator's Name

_____

Operator's Signature

_____

Supervisor's Name

_____

Supervisor's Signature

_____

PROPANE FORKLIFT INSPECTION CHECKLIST

Date: _____ Shift: _____

Forklift Serial Number: _____

Hour Meter Start: _____ End: _____ Total Hours: _____

	Gas gauge		Hour Meter
	LPG tank and locator pin		Hydraulic Controls
	LPG tank hose		Lights - Head and Tail
	Accelerator		Lights - Warning
	Alarms		Mast
	Battery Connector		Oil Leaks
	Belt		Oil Pressure
	Brakes - Parking		Overhead Guard
	Engine Oil Level		Radiator Level
	Forks		Safety Equipment
	Fuel		Steering
	Gauges		Tires
	Horn		Unusual Noises
	Hoses		Other: _____

Notes: _____
_____
_____
_____
_____
_____

Operator's Name

_____

Operator's Signature

_____

Supervisor's Name

_____

Supervisor's Signature

_____

PROPANE FORKLIFT INSPECTION CHECKLIST

Date: _____ Shift: _____

Forklift Serial Number: _____

Hour Meter Start:_____ End:_____ Total Hours:_____

	Gas gauge		Hour Meter
	LPG tank and locator pin		Hydraulic Controls
	LPG tank hose		Lights - Head and Tail
	Accelerator		Lights - Warning
	Alarms		Mast
	Battery Connector		Oil Leaks
	Belt		Oil Pressure
	Brakes - Parking		Overhead Guard
	Engine Oil Level		Radiator Level
	Forks		Safety Equipment
	Fuel		Steering
	Gauges		Tires
	Horn		Unusual Noises
	Hoses		Other: _____

Notes: _____
_____
_____
_____
_____
_____

Operator's Name	Supervisor's Name
_____	_____
Operator's Signature	Supervisor's Signature
_____	_____

PROPANE FORKLIFT INSPECTION CHECKLIST

Date: _____ Shift: _____

Forklift Serial Number: _____

Hour Meter Start: _____ End: _____ Total Hours: _____

	Gas gauge		Hour Meter
	LPG tank and locator pin		Hydraulic Controls
	LPG tank hose		Lights - Head and Tail
	Accelerator		Lights - Warning
	Alarms		Mast
	Battery Connector		Oil Leaks
	Belt		Oil Pressure
	Brakes - Parking		Overhead Guard
	Engine Oil Level		Radiator Level
	Forks		Safety Equipment
	Fuel		Steering
	Gauges		Tires
	Horn		Unusual Noises
	Hoses		Other: _____

Notes: _____
_____
_____
_____
_____
_____
_____

Operator's Name
_____
Operator's Signature
_____

Supervisor's Name
_____
Supervisor's Signature
_____

PROPANE FORKLIFT INSPECTION CHECKLIST

Date: _____ Shift: _____

Forklift Serial Number: _____

Hour Meter Start:_____ End:_____ Total Hours:_____

	Gas gauge		Hour Meter
	LPG tank and locator pin		Hydraulic Controls
	LPG tank hose		Lights - Head and Tail
	Accelerator		Lights - Warning
	Alarms		Mast
	Battery Connector		Oil Leaks
	Belt		Oil Pressure
	Brakes - Parking		Overhead Guard
	Engine Oil Level		Radiator Level
	Forks		Safety Equipment
	Fuel		Steering
	Gauges		Tires
	Horn		Unusual Noises
	Hoses		Other: _____

Notes: _____
_____
_____
_____
_____
_____

Operator's Name	Supervisor's Name
_____	_____
Operator's Signature	Supervisor's Signature
_____	_____

PROPANE FORKLIFT INSPECTION CHECKLIST

Date: _____ Shift: _____

Forklift Serial Number: _____

Hour Meter Start: _____ End: _____ Total Hours: _____

	Gas gauge		Hour Meter
	LPG tank and locator pin		Hydraulic Controls
	LPG tank hose		Lights - Head and Tail
	Accelerator		Lights - Warning
	Alarms		Mast
	Battery Connector		Oil Leaks
	Belt		Oil Pressure
	Brakes - Parking		Overhead Guard
	Engine Oil Level		Radiator Level
	Forks		Safety Equipment
	Fuel		Steering
	Gauges		Tires
	Horn		Unusual Noises
	Hoses		Other: _____

Notes: _____

_____

_____

_____

_____

_____

Operator's Name

_____

Operator's Signature

_____

Supervisor's Name

_____

Supervisor's Signature

_____

PROPANE FORKLIFT INSPECTION CHECKLIST

Date: _____ Shift: _____

Forklift Serial Number: _____

Hour Meter Start: _____ End: _____ Total Hours: _____

	Gas gauge		Hour Meter
	LPG tank and locator pin		Hydraulic Controls
	LPG tank hose		Lights - Head and Tail
	Accelerator		Lights - Warning
	Alarms		Mast
	Battery Connector		Oil Leaks
	Belt		Oil Pressure
	Brakes - Parking		Overhead Guard
	Engine Oil Level		Radiator Level
	Forks		Safety Equipment
	Fuel		Steering
	Gauges		Tires
	Horn		Unusual Noises
	Hoses		Other: _____

Notes: _____
_____
_____
_____
_____
_____

Operator's Name

_____

Operator's Signature

_____

Supervisor's Name

_____

Supervisor's Signature

_____

PROPANE FORKLIFT INSPECTION CHECKLIST

Date: _____ Shift: _____

Forklift Serial Number: _____

Hour Meter Start: _____ End: _____ Total Hours: _____

	Gas gauge		Hour Meter
	LPG tank and locator pin		Hydraulic Controls
	LPG tank hose		Lights - Head and Tail
	Accelerator		Lights - Warning
	Alarms		Mast
	Battery Connector		Oil Leaks
	Belt		Oil Pressure
	Brakes - Parking		Overhead Guard
	Engine Oil Level		Radiator Level
	Forks		Safety Equipment
	Fuel		Steering
	Gauges		Tires
	Horn		Unusual Noises
	Hoses		Other: _____

Notes: _____
_____
_____
_____
_____
_____

Operator's Name	Supervisor's Name
_____	_____
Operator's Signature	Supervisor's Signature
_____	_____

PROPANE FORKLIFT INSPECTION CHECKLIST

Date: _____ Shift: _____

Forklift Serial Number: _____

Hour Meter Start: _____ End: _____ Total Hours: _____

Gas gauge		Hour Meter
LPG tank and locator pin		Hydraulic Controls
LPG tank hose		Lights - Head and Tail
Accelerator		Lights - Warning
Alarms		Mast
Battery Connector		Oil Leaks
Belt		Oil Pressure
Brakes - Parking		Overhead Guard
Engine Oil Level		Radiator Level
Forks		Safety Equipment
Fuel		Steering
Gauges		Tires
Horn		Unusual Noises
Hoses		Other: _____

Notes: _____
_____
_____
_____
_____
_____

Operator's Name

_____

Operator's Signature

_____

Supervisor's Name

_____

Supervisor's Signature

_____

PROPANE FORKLIFT INSPECTION CHECKLIST

Date: _____ Shift: _____

Forklift Serial Number: _____

Hour Meter Start: _____ End: _____ Total Hours: _____

	Gas gauge		Hour Meter
	LPG tank and locator pin		Hydraulic Controls
	LPG tank hose		Lights - Head and Tail
	Accelerator		Lights - Warning
	Alarms		Mast
	Battery Connector		Oil Leaks
	Belt		Oil Pressure
	Brakes - Parking		Overhead Guard
	Engine Oil Level		Radiator Level
	Forks		Safety Equipment
	Fuel		Steering
	Gauges		Tires
	Horn		Unusual Noises
	Hoses		Other: _____

Notes: _____
_____
_____
_____
_____
_____

Operator's Name

_____

Operator's Signature

_____

Supervisor's Name

_____

Supervisor's Signature

_____

PROPANE FORKLIFT INSPECTION CHECKLIST

Date: _____ Shift: _____

Forklift Serial Number: _____

Hour Meter Start: _____ End: _____ Total Hours: _____

	Gas gauge		Hour Meter
	LPG tank and locator pin		Hydraulic Controls
	LPG tank hose		Lights - Head and Tail
	Accelerator		Lights - Warning
	Alarms		Mast
	Battery Connector		Oil Leaks
	Belt		Oil Pressure
	Brakes - Parking		Overhead Guard
	Engine Oil Level		Radiator Level
	Forks		Safety Equipment
	Fuel		Steering
	Gauges		Tires
	Horn		Unusual Noises
	Hoses		Other: _____

Notes: _____
_____
_____
_____
_____
_____

Operator's Name	Supervisor's Name
_____	_____
Operator's Signature	Supervisor's Signature
_____	_____

PROPANE FORKLIFT INSPECTION CHECKLIST

Date: _____ Shift: _____

Forklift Serial Number: _____

Hour Meter Start:_____ End:_____ Total Hours:_____

	Gas gauge		Hour Meter
	LPG tank and locator pin		Hydraulic Controls
	LPG tank hose		Lights - Head and Tail
	Accelerator		Lights - Warning
	Alarms		Mast
	Battery Connector		Oil Leaks
	Belt		Oil Pressure
	Brakes - Parking		Overhead Guard
	Engine Oil Level		Radiator Level
	Forks		Safety Equipment
	Fuel		Steering
	Gauges		Tires
	Horn		Unusual Noises
	Hoses		Other: _____

Notes: _____
_____
_____
_____
_____
_____

Operator's Name	Supervisor's Name
_____	_____
Operator's Signature	Supervisor's Signature
_____	_____

PROPANE FORKLIFT INSPECTION CHECKLIST

Date: _____ Shift: _____

Forklift Serial Number: _____

Hour Meter Start: _____ End: _____ Total Hours: _____

	Gas gauge		Hour Meter
	LPG tank and locator pin		Hydraulic Controls
	LPG tank hose		Lights - Head and Tail
	Accelerator		Lights - Warning
	Alarms		Mast
	Battery Connector		Oil Leaks
	Belt		Oil Pressure
	Brakes - Parking		Overhead Guard
	Engine Oil Level		Radiator Level
	Forks		Safety Equipment
	Fuel		Steering
	Gauges		Tires
	Horn		Unusual Noises
	Hoses		Other: _____

Notes: _____

_____

_____

_____

_____

_____

Operator's Name

_____

Operator's Signature

_____

Supervisor's Name

_____

Supervisor's Signature

_____

PROPANE FORKLIFT INSPECTION CHECKLIST

Date: _____ Shift: _____

Forklift Serial Number: _____

Hour Meter Start: _____ End: _____ Total Hours: _____

	Gas gauge		Hour Meter
	LPG tank and locator pin		Hydraulic Controls
	LPG tank hose		Lights - Head and Tail
	Accelerator		Lights - Warning
	Alarms		Mast
	Battery Connector		Oil Leaks
	Belt		Oil Pressure
	Brakes - Parking		Overhead Guard
	Engine Oil Level		Radiator Level
	Forks		Safety Equipment
	Fuel		Steering
	Gauges		Tires
	Horn		Unusual Noises
	Hoses		Other: _____

Notes: _____
_____
_____
_____
_____
_____

Operator's Name

_____

Operator's Signature

_____

Supervisor's Name

_____

Supervisor's Signature

_____

PROPANE FORKLIFT INSPECTION CHECKLIST

Date: _____ Shift: _____

Forklift Serial Number: _____

Hour Meter Start:_____ End:_____ Total Hours:_____

	Gas gauge		Hour Meter
	LPG tank and locator pin		Hydraulic Controls
	LPG tank hose		Lights - Head and Tail
	Accelerator		Lights - Warning
	Alarms		Mast
	Battery Connector		Oil Leaks
	Belt		Oil Pressure
	Brakes - Parking		Overhead Guard
	Engine Oil Level		Radiator Level
	Forks		Safety Equipment
	Fuel		Steering
	Gauges		Tires
	Horn		Unusual Noises
	Hoses		Other: _____

Notes: _____
_____
_____
_____
_____
_____
_____

Operator's Name

_____

Operator's Signature

_____

Supervisor's Name

_____

Supervisor's Signature

_____

PROPANE FORKLIFT INSPECTION CHECKLIST

Date: _____ Shift: _____

Forklift Serial Number: _____

Hour Meter Start: _____ End: _____ Total Hours: _____

Gas gauge	Hour Meter
LPG tank and locator pin	Hydraulic Controls
LPG tank hose	Lights - Head and Tail
Accelerator	Lights - Warning
Alarms	Mast
Battery Connector	Oil Leaks
Belt	Oil Pressure
Brakes - Parking	Overhead Guard
Engine Oil Level	Radiator Level
Forks	Safety Equipment
Fuel	Steering
Gauges	Tires
Horn	Unusual Noises
Hoses	Other: _____

Notes: _____
_____
_____
_____
_____
_____

Operator's Name	Supervisor's Name
_____	_____
Operator's Signature	Supervisor's Signature
_____	_____

PROPANE FORKLIFT INSPECTION CHECKLIST

Date: _____ Shift: _____

Forklift Serial Number: _____

Hour Meter Start: _____ End: _____ Total Hours: _____

	Gas gauge		Hour Meter
	LPG tank and locator pin		Hydraulic Controls
	LPG tank hose		Lights - Head and Tail
	Accelerator		Lights - Warning
	Alarms		Mast
	Battery Connector		Oil Leaks
	Belt		Oil Pressure
	Brakes - Parking		Overhead Guard
	Engine Oil Level		Radiator Level
	Forks		Safety Equipment
	Fuel		Steering
	Gauges		Tires
	Horn		Unusual Noises
	Hoses		Other: _____

Notes: _____
_____
_____
_____
_____
_____

Operator's Name	Supervisor's Name
_____	_____
Operator's Signature	Supervisor's Signature
_____	_____

PROPANE FORKLIFT INSPECTION CHECKLIST

Date: _____ Shift: _____

Forklift Serial Number: _____

Hour Meter Start: _____ End: _____ Total Hours: _____

	Gas gauge		Hour Meter
	LPG tank and locator pin		Hydraulic Controls
	LPG tank hose		Lights - Head and Tail
	Accelerator		Lights - Warning
	Alarms		Mast
	Battery Connector		Oil Leaks
	Belt		Oil Pressure
	Brakes - Parking		Overhead Guard
	Engine Oil Level		Radiator Level
	Forks		Safety Equipment
	Fuel		Steering
	Gauges		Tires
	Horn		Unusual Noises
	Hoses		Other: _____

Notes: _____
_____
_____
_____
_____
_____

Operator's Name	Supervisor's Name
_____	_____
Operator's Signature	Supervisor's Signature
_____	_____

PROPANE FORKLIFT INSPECTION CHECKLIST

Date: _____ Shift: _____

Forklift Serial Number: _____

Hour Meter Start: _____ End: _____ Total Hours: _____

	Gas gauge			Hour Meter
	LPG tank and locator pin			Hydraulic Controls
	LPG tank hose			Lights - Head and Tail
	Accelerator			Lights - Warning
	Alarms			Mast
	Battery Connector			Oil Leaks
	Belt			Oil Pressure
	Brakes - Parking			Overhead Guard
	Engine Oil Level			Radiator Level
	Forks			Safety Equipment
	Fuel			Steering
	Gauges			Tires
	Horn			Unusual Noises
	Hoses			Other: _____

Notes: _____
_____
_____
_____
_____
_____

Operator's Name	Supervisor's Name
_____	_____
Operator's Signature	Supervisor's Signature
_____	_____

PROPANE FORKLIFT INSPECTION CHECKLIST

Date: _____ Shift: _____

Forklift Serial Number: _____

Hour Meter Start: _____ End: _____ Total Hours: _____

	Gas gauge		Hour Meter
	LPG tank and locator pin		Hydraulic Controls
	LPG tank hose		Lights - Head and Tail
	Accelerator		Lights - Warning
	Alarms		Mast
	Battery Connector		Oil Leaks
	Belt		Oil Pressure
	Brakes - Parking		Overhead Guard
	Engine Oil Level		Radiator Level
	Forks		Safety Equipment
	Fuel		Steering
	Gauges		Tires
	Horn		Unusual Noises
	Hoses		Other: _____

Notes: _____
_____
_____
_____
_____
_____

Operator's Name	Supervisor's Name
_____	_____
Operator's Signature	Supervisor's Signature
_____	_____

PROPANE FORKLIFT INSPECTION CHECKLIST

Date: _____ Shift: _____

Forklift Serial Number: _____

Hour Meter Start: _____ End: _____ Total Hours: _____

	Gas gauge		Hour Meter
	LPG tank and locator pin		Hydraulic Controls
	LPG tank hose		Lights - Head and Tail
	Accelerator		Lights - Warning
	Alarms		Mast
	Battery Connector		Oil Leaks
	Belt		Oil Pressure
	Brakes - Parking		Overhead Guard
	Engine Oil Level		Radiator Level
	Forks		Safety Equipment
	Fuel		Steering
	Gauges		Tires
	Horn		Unusual Noises
	Hoses		Other: _____

Notes: _____

_____

_____

_____

_____

_____

_____

Operator's Name	Supervisor's Name
_____	_____
Operator's Signature	Supervisor's Signature
_____	_____

PROPANE FORKLIFT INSPECTION CHECKLIST

Date: _____ Shift: _____

Forklift Serial Number: _____

Hour Meter Start: _____ End: _____ Total Hours: _____

	Gas gauge		Hour Meter
	LPG tank and locator pin		Hydraulic Controls
	LPG tank hose		Lights - Head and Tail
	Accelerator		Lights - Warning
	Alarms		Mast
	Battery Connector		Oil Leaks
	Belt		Oil Pressure
	Brakes - Parking		Overhead Guard
	Engine Oil Level		Radiator Level
	Forks		Safety Equipment
	Fuel		Steering
	Gauges		Tires
	Horn		Unusual Noises
	Hoses		Other: _____

Notes: _____
_____
_____
_____
_____
_____

Operator's Name	Supervisor's Name
_____	_____
Operator's Signature	Supervisor's Signature
_____	_____

PROPANE FORKLIFT INSPECTION CHECKLIST

Date: _____ Shift: _____

Forklift Serial Number: _____

Hour Meter Start: _____ End: _____ Total Hours: _____

	Gas gauge		Hour Meter
	LPG tank and locator pin		Hydraulic Controls
	LPG tank hose		Lights - Head and Tail
	Accelerator		Lights - Warning
	Alarms		Mast
	Battery Connector		Oil Leaks
	Belt		Oil Pressure
	Brakes - Parking		Overhead Guard
	Engine Oil Level		Radiator Level
	Forks		Safety Equipment
	Fuel		Steering
	Gauges		Tires
	Horn		Unusual Noises
	Hoses		Other: _____

Notes: _____
_____
_____
_____
_____
_____

Operator's Name	Supervisor's Name
_____	_____
Operator's Signature	Supervisor's Signature
_____	_____

PROPANE FORKLIFT INSPECTION CHECKLIST

Date: _____ Shift: _____

Forklift Serial Number: _____

Hour Meter Start: _____ End: _____ Total Hours: _____

	Gas gauge		Hour Meter
	LPG tank and locator pin		Hydraulic Controls
	LPG tank hose		Lights - Head and Tail
	Accelerator		Lights - Warning
	Alarms		Mast
	Battery Connector		Oil Leaks
	Belt		Oil Pressure
	Brakes - Parking		Overhead Guard
	Engine Oil Level		Radiator Level
	Forks		Safety Equipment
	Fuel		Steering
	Gauges		Tires
	Horn		Unusual Noises
	Hoses		Other: _____

Notes: _____
_____
_____
_____
_____
_____

Operator's Name	Supervisor's Name
_____	_____
Operator's Signature	Supervisor's Signature
_____	_____

PROPANE FORKLIFT INSPECTION CHECKLIST

Date: _____ Shift: _____

Forklift Serial Number: _____

Hour Meter Start: _____ End: _____ Total Hours: _____

	Gas gauge		Hour Meter
	LPG tank and locator pin		Hydraulic Controls
	LPG tank hose		Lights - Head and Tail
	Accelerator		Lights - Warning
	Alarms		Mast
	Battery Connector		Oil Leaks
	Belt		Oil Pressure
	Brakes - Parking		Overhead Guard
	Engine Oil Level		Radiator Level
	Forks		Safety Equipment
	Fuel		Steering
	Gauges		Tires
	Horn		Unusual Noises
	Hoses		Other: _____

Notes: _____
_____
_____
_____
_____
_____

Operator's Name	Supervisor's Name
_____	_____
Operator's Signature	Supervisor's Signature
_____	_____

PROPANE FORKLIFT INSPECTION CHECKLIST

Date: _____ Shift: _____

Forklift Serial Number: _____

Hour Meter Start: _____ End: _____ Total Hours: _____

	Gas gauge		Hour Meter
	LPG tank and locator pin		Hydraulic Controls
	LPG tank hose		Lights - Head and Tail
	Accelerator		Lights - Warning
	Alarms		Mast
	Battery Connector		Oil Leaks
	Belt		Oil Pressure
	Brakes - Parking		Overhead Guard
	Engine Oil Level		Radiator Level
	Forks		Safety Equipment
	Fuel		Steering
	Gauges		Tires
	Horn		Unusual Noises
	Hoses		Other: _____

Notes: _____
_____
_____
_____
_____
_____

Operator's Name	Supervisor's Name
_____	_____
Operator's Signature	Supervisor's Signature
_____	_____

PROPANE FORKLIFT INSPECTION CHECKLIST

Date: _____ Shift: _____

Forklift Serial Number: _____

Hour Meter Start: _____ End: _____ Total Hours: _____

	Gas gauge		Hour Meter
	LPG tank and locator pin		Hydraulic Controls
	LPG tank hose		Lights - Head and Tail
	Accelerator		Lights - Warning
	Alarms		Mast
	Battery Connector		Oil Leaks
	Belt		Oil Pressure
	Brakes - Parking		Overhead Guard
	Engine Oil Level		Radiator Level
	Forks		Safety Equipment
	Fuel		Steering
	Gauges		Tires
	Horn		Unusual Noises
	Hoses		Other: _____

Notes: _____
_____
_____
_____
_____
_____
_____

Operator's Name

_____

Operator's Signature

_____

Supervisor's Name

_____

Supervisor's Signature

_____

PROPANE FORKLIFT INSPECTION CHECKLIST

Date: _____ Shift: _____

Forklift Serial Number: _____

Hour Meter Start: _____ End: _____ Total Hours: _____

	Gas gauge		Hour Meter
	LPG tank and locator pin		Hydraulic Controls
	LPG tank hose		Lights - Head and Tail
	Accelerator		Lights - Warning
	Alarms		Mast
	Battery Connector		Oil Leaks
	Belt		Oil Pressure
	Brakes - Parking		Overhead Guard
	Engine Oil Level		Radiator Level
	Forks		Safety Equipment
	Fuel		Steering
	Gauges		Tires
	Horn		Unusual Noises
	Hoses		Other: _____

Notes: _____
_____
_____
_____
_____
_____

Operator's Name	Supervisor's Name
_____	_____
Operator's Signature	Supervisor's Signature
_____	_____

PROPANE FORKLIFT INSPECTION CHECKLIST

Date: _____ Shift: _____

Forklift Serial Number: _____

Hour Meter Start: _____ End: _____ Total Hours: _____

	Gas gauge		Hour Meter
	LPG tank and locator pin		Hydraulic Controls
	LPG tank hose		Lights - Head and Tail
	Accelerator		Lights - Warning
	Alarms		Mast
	Battery Connector		Oil Leaks
	Belt		Oil Pressure
	Brakes - Parking		Overhead Guard
	Engine Oil Level		Radiator Level
	Forks		Safety Equipment
	Fuel		Steering
	Gauges		Tires
	Horn		Unusual Noises
	Hoses		Other: _____

Notes: _____
_____
_____
_____
_____
_____

Operator's Name	Supervisor's Name
_____	_____
Operator's Signature	Supervisor's Signature
_____	_____

PROPANE FORKLIFT INSPECTION CHECKLIST

Date: _____ Shift: _____

Forklift Serial Number: _____

Hour Meter Start: _____ End: _____ Total Hours: _____

	Gas gauge		Hour Meter
	LPG tank and locator pin		Hydraulic Controls
	LPG tank hose		Lights - Head and Tail
	Accelerator		Lights - Warning
	Alarms		Mast
	Battery Connector		Oil Leaks
	Belt		Oil Pressure
	Brakes - Parking		Overhead Guard
	Engine Oil Level		Radiator Level
	Forks		Safety Equipment
	Fuel		Steering
	Gauges		Tires
	Horn		Unusual Noises
	Hoses		Other: _____

Notes: _____
_____
_____
_____
_____
_____

Operator's Name	Supervisor's Name
_____	_____
Operator's Signature	Supervisor's Signature
_____	_____

PROPANE FORKLIFT INSPECTION CHECKLIST

Date: _____ Shift: _____

Forklift Serial Number: _____

Hour Meter Start: _____ End: _____ Total Hours: _____

	Gas gauge		Hour Meter
	LPG tank and locator pin		Hydraulic Controls
	LPG tank hose		Lights - Head and Tail
	Accelerator		Lights - Warning
	Alarms		Mast
	Battery Connector		Oil Leaks
	Belt		Oil Pressure
	Brakes - Parking		Overhead Guard
	Engine Oil Level		Radiator Level
	Forks		Safety Equipment
	Fuel		Steering
	Gauges		Tires
	Horn		Unusual Noises
	Hoses		Other: _____

Notes: _____
_____
_____
_____
_____
_____
_____

Operator's Name

_____

Operator's Signature

_____

Supervisor's Name

_____

Supervisor's Signature

_____

PROPANE FORKLIFT INSPECTION CHECKLIST

Date: _____ Shift: _____

Forklift Serial Number: _____

Hour Meter Start: _____ End: _____ Total Hours: _____

	Gas gauge		Hour Meter
	LPG tank and locator pin		Hydraulic Controls
	LPG tank hose		Lights - Head and Tail
	Accelerator		Lights - Warning
	Alarms		Mast
	Battery Connector		Oil Leaks
	Belt		Oil Pressure
	Brakes - Parking		Overhead Guard
	Engine Oil Level		Radiator Level
	Forks		Safety Equipment
	Fuel		Steering
	Gauges		Tires
	Horn		Unusual Noises
	Hoses		Other: _____

Notes: _____
_____
_____
_____
_____
_____

Operator's Name

_____

Operator's Signature

_____

Supervisor's Name

_____

Supervisor's Signature

_____

PROPANE FORKLIFT INSPECTION CHECKLIST

Date: _____ Shift: _____

Forklift Serial Number: _____

Hour Meter Start: _____ End: _____ Total Hours: _____

	Gas gauge		Hour Meter
	LPG tank and locator pin		Hydraulic Controls
	LPG tank hose		Lights - Head and Tail
	Accelerator		Lights - Warning
	Alarms		Mast
	Battery Connector		Oil Leaks
	Belt		Oil Pressure
	Brakes - Parking		Overhead Guard
	Engine Oil Level		Radiator Level
	Forks		Safety Equipment
	Fuel		Steering
	Gauges		Tires
	Horn		Unusual Noises
	Hoses		Other: _____

Notes: _____
_____
_____
_____
_____
_____

Operator's Name
_____

Operator's Signature
_____

Supervisor's Name
_____

Supervisor's Signature
_____

PROPANE FORKLIFT INSPECTION CHECKLIST

Date: _____ Shift: _____

Forklift Serial Number: _____

Hour Meter Start: _____ End: _____ Total Hours: _____

	Gas gauge		Hour Meter
	LPG tank and locator pin		Hydraulic Controls
	LPG tank hose		Lights - Head and Tail
	Accelerator		Lights - Warning
	Alarms		Mast
	Battery Connector		Oil Leaks
	Belt		Oil Pressure
	Brakes - Parking		Overhead Guard
	Engine Oil Level		Radiator Level
	Forks		Safety Equipment
	Fuel		Steering
	Gauges		Tires
	Horn		Unusual Noises
	Hoses		Other: _____

Notes: _____

_____

_____

_____

_____

_____

Operator's Name

_____

Operator's Signature

_____

Supervisor's Name

_____

Supervisor's Signature

_____

PROPANE FORKLIFT INSPECTION CHECKLIST

Date: _____ Shift: _____

Forklift Serial Number: _____

Hour Meter Start: _____ End: _____ Total Hours: _____

	Gas gauge		Hour Meter
	LPG tank and locator pin		Hydraulic Controls
	LPG tank hose		Lights Head and Tail
	Accelerator		Lights - Warning
	Alarms		Mast
	Battery Connector		Oil Leaks
	Belt		Oil Pressure
	Brakes - Parking		Overhead Guard
	Engine Oil Level		Radiator Level
	Forks		Safety Equipment
	Fuel		Steering
	Gauges		Tires
	Horn		Unusual Noises
	Hoses		Other: _____

Notes: _____
_____
_____
_____
_____
_____

Operator's Name	Supervisor's Name
_____	_____
Operator's Signature	Supervisor's Signature
_____	_____

PROPANE FORKLIFT INSPECTION CHECKLIST

Date: _____ Shift: _____

Forklift Serial Number: _____

Hour Meter Start: _____ End: _____ Total Hours: _____

	Gas gauge		Hour Meter
	LPG tank and locator pin		Hydraulic Controls
	LPG tank hose		Lights - Head and Tail
	Accelerator		Lights - Warning
	Alarms		Mast
	Battery Connector		Oil Leaks
	Belt		Oil Pressure
	Brakes - Parking		Overhead Guard
	Engine Oil Level		Radiator Level
	Forks		Safety Equipment
	Fuel		Steering
	Gauges		Tires
	Horn		Unusual Noises
	Hoses		Other: _____

Notes: _____
_____
_____
_____
_____
_____

Operator's Name	Supervisor's Name
_____	_____
Operator's Signature	Supervisor's Signature
_____	_____

PROPANE FORKLIFT INSPECTION CHECKLIST

Date: _____ Shift: _____

Forklift Serial Number: _____

Hour Meter Start: _____ End: _____ Total Hours: _____

	Gas gauge		Hour Meter
	LPG tank and locator pin		Hydraulic Controls
	LPG tank hose		Lights - Head and Tail
	Accelerator		Lights - Warning
	Alarms		Mast
	Battery Connector		Oil Leaks
	Belt		Oil Pressure
	Brakes - Parking		Overhead Guard
	Engine Oil Level		Radiator Level
	Forks		Safety Equipment
	Fuel		Steering
	Gauges		Tires
	Horn		Unusual Noises
	Hoses		Other: _____

Notes: _____
_____
_____
_____
_____
_____

Operator's Name	Supervisor's Name
_____	_____
Operator's Signature	Supervisor's Signature
_____	_____

PROPANE FORKLIFT INSPECTION CHECKLIST

Date: _____ Shift: _____

Forklift Serial Number: _____

Hour Meter Start: _____ End: _____ Total Hours: _____

	Gas gauge			Hour Meter
	LPG tank and locator pin			Hydraulic Controls
	LPG tank hose			Lights - Head and Tail
	Accelerator			Lights - Warning
	Alarms			Mast
	Battery Connector			Oil Leaks
	Belt			Oil Pressure
	Brakes - Parking			Overhead Guard
	Engine Oil Level			Radiator Level
	Forks			Safety Equipment
	Fuel			Steering
	Gauges			Tires
	Horn			Unusual Noises
	Hoses			Other: _____

Notes: _____

_____

_____

_____

_____

_____

Operator's Name

_____

Operator's Signature

_____

Supervisor's Name

_____

Supervisor's Signature

_____

PROPANE FORKLIFT INSPECTION CHECKLIST

Date: _____ Shift: _____

Forklift Serial Number: _____

Hour Meter Start: _____ End: _____ Total Hours: _____

	Gas gauge		Hour Meter
	LPG tank and locator pin		Hydraulic Controls
	LPG tank hose		Lights - Head and Tail
	Accelerator		Lights - Warning
	Alarms		Mast
	Battery Connector		Oil Leaks
	Belt		Oil Pressure
	Brakes - Parking		Overhead Guard
	Engine Oil Level		Radiator Level
	Forks		Safety Equipment
	Fuel		Steering
	Gauges		Tires
	Horn		Unusual Noises
	Hoses		Other: _____

Notes: _____
_____
_____
_____
_____
_____
_____

Operator's Name

_____

Operator's Signature

_____

Supervisor's Name

_____

Supervisor's Signature

_____

PROPANE FORKLIFT INSPECTION CHECKLIST

Date: _____ Shift: _____

Forklift Serial Number: _____

Hour Meter Start: _____ End: _____ Total Hours: _____

	Gas gauge		Hour Meter
	LPG tank and locator pin		Hydraulic Controls
	LPG tank hose		Lights - Head and Tail
	Accelerator		Lights - Warning
	Alarms		Mast
	Battery Connector		Oil Leaks
	Belt		Oil Pressure
	Brakes - Parking		Overhead Guard
	Engine Oil Level		Radiator Level
	Forks		Safety Equipment
	Fuel		Steering
	Gauges		Tires
	Horn		Unusual Noises
	Hoses		Other: _____

Notes: _____
_____
_____
_____
_____
_____

Operator's Name	Supervisor's Name
_____	_____
Operator's Signature	Supervisor's Signature
_____	_____

PROPANE FORKLIFT INSPECTION CHECKLIST

Date: _____ Shift: _____

Forklift Serial Number: _____

Hour Meter Start: _____ End: _____ Total Hours: _____

	Gas gauge		Hour Meter
	LPG tank and locator pin		Hydraulic Controls
	LPG tank hose		Lights - Head and Tail
	Accelerator		Lights - Warning
	Alarms		Mast
	Battery Connector		Oil Leaks
	Belt		Oil Pressure
	Brakes - Parking		Overhead Guard
	Engine Oil Level		Radiator Level
	Forks		Safety Equipment
	Fuel		Steering
	Gauges		Tires
	Horn		Unusual Noises
	Hoses		Other: _____

Notes: _____
_____
_____
_____
_____
_____

Operator's Name	Supervisor's Name
_____	_____
Operator's Signature	Supervisor's Signature
_____	_____

PROPANE FORKLIFT INSPECTION CHECKLIST

Date: _____ Shift: _____

Forklift Serial Number: _____

Hour Meter Start: _____ End: _____ Total Hours: _____

	Gas gauge		Hour Meter
	LPG tank and locator pin		Hydraulic Controls
	LPG tank hose		Lights - Head and Tail
	Accelerator		Lights - Warning
	Alarms		Mast
	Battery Connector		Oil Leaks
	Belt		Oil Pressure
	Brakes - Parking		Overhead Guard
	Engine Oil Level		Radiator Level
	Forks		Safety Equipment
	Fuel		Steering
	Gauges		Tires
	Horn		Unusual Noises
	Hoses		Other: _____

Notes: _____
_____
_____
_____
_____
_____

Operator's Name
_____

Operator's Signature
_____

Supervisor's Name
_____

Supervisor's Signature
_____

PROPANE FORKLIFT INSPECTION CHECKLIST

Date: _____ Shift: _____

Forklift Serial Number: _____

Hour Meter Start: _____ End: _____ Total Hours: _____

	Gas gauge		Hour Meter
	LPG tank and locator pin		Hydraulic Controls
	LPG tank hose		Lights - Head and Tail
	Accelerator		Lights - Warning
	Alarms		Mast
	Battery Connector		Oil Leaks
	Belt		Oil Pressure
	Brakes - Parking		Overhead Guard
	Engine Oil Level		Radiator Level
	Forks		Safety Equipment
	Fuel		Steering
	Gauges		Tires
	Horn		Unusual Noises
	Hoses		Other: _____

Notes: _____
_____
_____
_____
_____
_____

Operator's Name

_____

Operator's Signature

_____

Supervisor's Name

_____

Supervisor's Signature

_____

PROPANE FORKLIFT INSPECTION CHECKLIST

Date: _____ Shift: _____

Forklift Serial Number: _____

Hour Meter Start: _____ End: _____ Total Hours: _____

	Gas gauge		Hour Meter
	LPG tank and locator pin		Hydraulic Controls
	LPG tank hose		Lights - Head and Tail
	Accelerator		Lights - Warning
	Alarms		Mast
	Battery Connector		Oil Leaks
	Belt		Oil Pressure
	Brakes - Parking		Overhead Guard
	Engine Oil Level		Radiator Level
	Forks		Safety Equipment
	Fuel		Steering
	Gauges		Tires
	Horn		Unusual Noises
	Hoses		Other: _____

Notes: _____
_____
_____
_____
_____
_____

Operator's Name	Supervisor's Name
_____	_____
Operator's Signature	Supervisor's Signature
_____	_____

PROPANE FORKLIFT INSPECTION CHECKLIST

Date: _____ Shift: _____

Forklift Serial Number: _____

Hour Meter Start: _____ End: _____ Total Hours: _____

	Gas gauge		Hour Meter
	LPG tank and locator pin		Hydraulic Controls
	LPG tank hose		Lights - Head and Tail
	Accelerator		Lights - Warning
	Alarms		Mast
	Battery Connector		Oil Leaks
	Belt		Oil Pressure
	Brakes - Parking		Overhead Guard
	Engine Oil Level		Radiator Level
	Forks		Safety Equipment
	Fuel		Steering
	Gauges		Tires
	Horn		Unusual Noises
	Hoses		Other: _____

Notes: _____
_____
_____
_____
_____
_____

Operator's Name	Supervisor's Name
_____	_____
Operator's Signature	Supervisor's Signature
_____	_____

PROPANE FORKLIFT INSPECTION CHECKLIST

Date: _____ Shift: _____

Forklift Serial Number: _____

Hour Meter Start: _____ End: _____ Total Hours: _____

	Gas gauge		Hour Meter
	LPG tank and locator pin		Hydraulic Controls
	LPG tank hose		Lights - Head and Tail
	Accelerator		Lights - Warning
	Alarms		Mast
	Battery Connector		Oil Leaks
	Belt		Oil Pressure
	Brakes - Parking		Overhead Guard
	Engine Oil Level		Radiator Level
	Forks		Safety Equipment
	Fuel		Steering
	Gauges		Tires
	Horn		Unusual Noises
	Hoses		Other: _____

Notes: _____

_____

_____

_____

_____

_____

Operator's Name	Supervisor's Name
_____	_____
Operator's Signature	Supervisor's Signature
_____	_____

PROPANE FORKLIFT INSPECTION CHECKLIST

Date: _____ Shift: _____

Forklift Serial Number: _____

Hour Meter Start: _____ End: _____ Total Hours: _____

Gas gauge		Hour Meter
LPG tank and locator pin		Hydraulic Controls
LPG tank hose		Lights - Head and Tail
Accelerator		Lights - Warning
Alarms		Mast
Battery Connector		Oil Leaks
Belt		Oil Pressure
Brakes - Parking		Overhead Guard
Engine Oil Level		Radiator Level
Forks		Safety Equipment
Fuel		Steering
Gauges		Tires
Horn		Unusual Noises
Hoses		Other: _____

Notes: _____
_____
_____
_____
_____
_____

Operator's Name	Supervisor's Name
_____	_____
Operator's Signature	Supervisor's Signature
_____	_____

PROPANE FORKLIFT INSPECTION CHECKLIST

Date: _____ Shift: _____

Forklift Serial Number: _____

Hour Meter Start: _____ End: _____ Total Hours: _____

	Gas gauge		Hour Meter
	LPG tank and locator pin		Hydraulic Controls
	LPG tank hose		Lights - Head and Tail
	Accelerator		Lights - Warning
	Alarms		Mast
	Battery Connector		Oil Leaks
	Belt		Oil Pressure
	Brakes - Parking		Overhead Guard
	Engine Oil Level		Radiator Level
	Forks		Safety Equipment
	Fuel		Steering
	Gauges		Tires
	Horn		Unusual Noises
	Hoses		Other: _____

Notes: _____

_____

_____

_____

_____

_____

Operator's Name	Supervisor's Name
_____	_____
Operator's Signature	Supervisor's Signature
_____	_____

PROPANE FORKLIFT INSPECTION CHECKLIST

Date: _____ Shift: _____

Forklift Serial Number: _____

Hour Meter Start: _____ End: _____ Total Hours: _____

	Gas gauge		Hour Meter
	LPG tank and locator pin		Hydraulic Controls
	LPG tank hose		Lights - Head and Tail
	Accelerator		Lights - Warning
	Alarms		Mast
	Battery Connector		Oil Leaks
	Belt		Oil Pressure
	Brakes - Parking		Overhead Guard
	Engine Oil Level		Radiator Level
	Forks		Safety Equipment
	Fuel		Steering
	Gauges		Tires
	Horn		Unusual Noises
	Hoses		Other: _____

Notes: _____
_____
_____
_____
_____
_____

Operator's Name	Supervisor's Name
_____	_____
Operator's Signature	Supervisor's Signature
_____	_____

PROPANE FORKLIFT INSPECTION CHECKLIST

Date: _____ Shift: _____

Forklift Serial Number: _____

Hour Meter Start: _____ End: _____ Total Hours: _____

	Gas gauge		Hour Meter
	LPG tank and locator pin		Hydraulic Controls
	LPG tank hose		Lights - Head and Tail
	Accelerator		Lights - Warning
	Alarms		Mast
	Battery Connector		Oil Leaks
	Belt		Oil Pressure
	Brakes - Parking		Overhead Guard
	Engine Oil Level		Radiator Level
	Forks		Safety Equipment
	Fuel		Steering
	Gauges		Tires
	Horn		Unusual Noises
	Hoses		Other: _____

Notes: _____
_____
_____
_____
_____
_____

Operator's Name

_____

Operator's Signature

_____

Supervisor's Name

_____

Supervisor's Signature

_____

PROPANE FORKLIFT INSPECTION CHECKLIST

Date: _____ Shift: _____

Forklift Serial Number: _____

Hour Meter Start:_____ End:_____ Total Hours:_____

Gas gauge		Hour Meter	
LPG tank and locator pin		Hydraulic Controls	
LPG tank hose		Lights - Head and Tail	
Accelerator		Lights - Warning	
Alarms		Mast	
Battery Connector		Oil Leaks	
Belt		Oil Pressure	
Brakes - Parking		Overhead Guard	
Engine Oil Level		Radiator Level	
Forks		Safety Equipment	
Fuel		Steering	
Gauges		Tires	
Horn		Unusual Noises	
Hoses		Other: _____	

Notes: _____
_____
_____
_____
_____
_____

Operator's Name
_____

Operator's Signature
_____

Supervisor's Name
_____

Supervisor's Signature
_____

PROPANE FORKLIFT INSPECTION CHECKLIST

Date: _____ Shift: _____

Forklift Serial Number: _____

Hour Meter Start: _____ End: _____ Total Hours: _____

Gas gauge		Hour Meter	
LPG tank and locator pin		Hydraulic Controls	
LPG tank hose		Lights - Head and Tail	
Accelerator		Lights - Warning	
Alarms		Mast	
Battery Connector		Oil Leaks	
Belt		Oil Pressure	
Brakes - Parking		Overhead Guard	
Engine Oil Level		Radiator Level	
Forks		Safety Equipment	
Fuel		Steering	
Gauges		Tires	
Horn		Unusual Noises	
Hoses		Other: _____	

Notes: _____
_____
_____
_____
_____
_____

Operator's Name	Supervisor's Name
_____	_____
Operator's Signature	Supervisor's Signature
_____	_____

PROPANE FORKLIFT INSPECTION CHECKLIST

Date: _____ Shift: _____

Forklift Serial Number: _____

Hour Meter Start: _____ End: _____ Total Hours: _____

	Gas gauge		Hour Meter
	LPG tank and locator pin		Hydraulic Controls
	LPG tank hose		Lights - Head and Tail
	Accelerator		Lights - Warning
	Alarms		Mast
	Battery Connector		Oil Leaks
	Belt		Oil Pressure
	Brakes - Parking		Overhead Guard
	Engine Oil Level		Radiator Level
	Forks		Safety Equipment
	Fuel		Steering
	Gauges		Tires
	Horn		Unusual Noises
	Hoses		Other: _____

Notes: _____
_____
_____
_____
_____
_____

Operator's Name	Supervisor's Name
_____	_____
Operator's Signature	Supervisor's Signature
_____	_____

PROPANE FORKLIFT INSPECTION CHECKLIST

Date: _____ Shift: _____

Forklift Serial Number: _____

Hour Meter Start: _____ End: _____ Total Hours: _____

	Gas gauge		Hour Meter
	LPG tank and locator pin		Hydraulic Controls
	LPG tank hose		Lights - Head and Tail
	Accelerator		Lights - Warning
	Alarms		Mast
	Battery Connector		Oil Leaks
	Belt		Oil Pressure
	Brakes - Parking		Overhead Guard
	Engine Oil Level		Radiator Level
	Forks		Safety Equipment
	Fuel		Steering
	Gauges		Tires
	Horn		Unusual Noises
	Hoses		Other: _____

Notes: _____

_____

_____

_____

_____

_____

Operator's Name	Supervisor's Name
_____	_____
Operator's Signature	Supervisor's Signature
_____	_____

PROPANE FORKLIFT INSPECTION CHECKLIST

Date: _____ Shift: _____

Forklift Serial Number: _____

Hour Meter Start: _____ End: _____ Total Hours: _____

	Gas gauge			Hour Meter
	LPG tank and locator pin			Hydraulic Controls
	LPG tank hose			Lights - Head and Tail
	Accelerator			Lights - Warning
	Alarms			Mast
	Battery Connector			Oil Leaks
	Belt			Oil Pressure
	Brakes - Parking			Overhead Guard
	Engine Oil Level			Radiator Level
	Forks			Safety Equipment
	Fuel			Steering
	Gauges			Tires
	Horn			Unusual Noises
	Hoses			Other: _____

Notes: _____
_____
_____
_____
_____
_____

Operator's Name
_____

Operator's Signature
_____

Supervisor's Name
_____

Supervisor's Signature
_____

PROPANE FORKLIFT INSPECTION CHECKLIST

Date: _____ Shift: _____

Forklift Serial Number: _____

Hour Meter Start: _____ End: _____ Total Hours: _____

Gas gauge	Hour Meter
LPG tank and locator pin	Hydraulic Controls
LPG tank hose	Lights - Head and Tail
Accelerator	Lights - Warning
Alarms	Mast
Battery Connector	Oil Leaks
Belt	Oil Pressure
Brakes - Parking	Overhead Guard
Engine Oil Level	Radiator Level
Forks	Safety Equipment
Fuel	Steering
Gauges	Tires
Horn	Unusual Noises
Hoses	Other: _____

Notes: _____
_____
_____
_____
_____
_____

Operator's Name	Supervisor's Name
_____	_____
Operator's Signature	Supervisor's Signature
_____	_____

PROPANE FORKLIFT INSPECTION CHECKLIST

Date: _____ Shift: _____

Forklift Serial Number: _____

Hour Meter Start: _____ End: _____ Total Hours: _____

	Gas gauge		Hour Meter
	LPG tank and locator pin		Hydraulic Controls
	LPG tank hose		Lights - Head and Tail
	Accelerator		Lights - Warning
	Alarms		Mast
	Battery Connector		Oil Leaks
	Belt		Oil Pressure
	Brakes - Parking		Overhead Guard
	Engine Oil Level		Radiator Level
	Forks		Safety Equipment
	Fuel		Steering
	Gauges		Tires
	Horn		Unusual Noises
	Hoses		Other: _____

Notes: _____
_____
_____
_____
_____
_____
_____

Operator's Name	Supervisor's Name
_____	_____
Operator's Signature	Supervisor's Signature
_____	_____

PROPANE FORKLIFT INSPECTION CHECKLIST

Date: _____ Shift: _____

Forklift Serial Number: _____

Hour Meter Start: _____ End: _____ Total Hours: _____

	Gas gauge		Hour Meter
	LPG tank and locator pin		Hydraulic Controls
	LPG tank hose		Lights - Head and Tail
	Accelerator		Lights - Warning
	Alarms		Mast
	Battery Connector		Oil Leaks
	Belt		Oil Pressure
	Brakes - Parking		Overhead Guard
	Engine Oil Level		Radiator Level
	Forks		Safety Equipment
	Fuel		Steering
	Gauges		Tires
	Horn		Unusual Noises
	Hoses		Other: _____

Notes: _____
_____
_____
_____
_____
_____
_____

Operator's Name

_____

Operator's Signature

_____

Supervisor's Name

_____

Supervisor's Signature

_____

PROPANE FORKLIFT INSPECTION CHECKLIST

Date: _____ Shift: _____

Forklift Serial Number: _____

Hour Meter Start: _____ End: _____ Total Hours: _____

	Gas gauge		Hour Meter
	LPG tank and locator pin		Hydraulic Controls
	LPG tank hose		Lights - Head and Tail
	Accelerator		Lights - Warning
	Alarms		Mast
	Battery Connector		Oil Leaks
	Belt		Oil Pressure
	Brakes - Parking		Overhead Guard
	Engine Oil Level		Radiator Level
	Forks		Safety Equipment
	Fuel		Steering
	Gauges		Tires
	Horn		Unusual Noises
	Hoses		Other: _____

Notes: _____
_____
_____
_____
_____
_____

Operator's Name	Supervisor's Name
_____	_____
Operator's Signature	Supervisor's Signature
_____	_____

PROPANE FORKLIFT INSPECTION CHECKLIST

Date: _____ Shift: _____

Forklift Serial Number: _____

Hour Meter Start:_____ End:_____ Total Hours:_____

Gas gauge		Hour Meter	
LPG tank and locator pin		Hydraulic Controls	
LPG tank hose		Lights - Head and Tail	
Accelerator		Lights - Warning	
Alarms		Mast	
Battery Connector		Oil Leaks	
Belt		Oil Pressure	
Brakes - Parking		Overhead Guard	
Engine Oil Level		Radiator Level	
Forks		Safety Equipment	
Fuel		Steering	
Gauges		Tires	
Horn		Unusual Noises	
Hoses		Other: _____	

Notes: _____
_____
_____
_____
_____
_____

Operator's Name	Supervisor's Name
_____	_____
Operator's Signature	Supervisor's Signature
_____	_____

PROPANE FORKLIFT INSPECTION CHECKLIST

Date: _____ Shift: _____

Forklift Serial Number: _____

Hour Meter Start: _____ End: _____ Total Hours: _____

	Gas gauge		Hour Meter
	LPG tank and locator pin		Hydraulic Controls
	LPG tank hose		Lights - Head and Tail
	Accelerator		Lights - Warning
	Alarms		Mast
	Battery Connector		Oil Leaks
	Belt		Oil Pressure
	Brakes - Parking		Overhead Guard
	Engine Oil Level		Radiator Level
	Forks		Safety Equipment
	Fuel		Steering
	Gauges		Tires
	Horn		Unusual Noises
	Hoses		Other: _____

Notes: _____
_____
_____
_____
_____
_____

Operator's Name

_____

Operator's Signature

_____

Supervisor's Name

_____

Supervisor's Signature

_____

PROPANE FORKLIFT INSPECTION CHECKLIST

Date: _____ Shift: _____

Forklift Serial Number: _____

Hour Meter Start:_____ End:_____ Total Hours:_____

	Gas gauge		Hour Meter
	LPG tank and locator pin		Hydraulic Controls
	LPG tank hose		Lights - Head and Tail
	Accelerator		Lights - Warning
	Alarms		Mast
	Battery Connector		Oil Leaks
	Belt		Oil Pressure
	Brakes - Parking		Overhead Guard
	Engine Oil Level		Radiator Level
	Forks		Safety Equipment
	Fuel		Steering
	Gauges		Tires
	Horn		Unusual Noises
	Hoses		Other: _____

Notes: _____
_____
_____
_____
_____
_____
_____

Operator's Name	Supervisor's Name
_____	_____
Operator's Signature	Supervisor's Signature
_____	_____

PROPANE FORKLIFT INSPECTION CHECKLIST

Date: _____ Shift: _____

Forklift Serial Number: _____

Hour Meter Start: _____ End: _____ Total Hours: _____

	Gas gauge		Hour Meter
	LPG tank and locator pin		Hydraulic Controls
	LPG tank hose		Lights - Head and Tail
	Accelerator		Lights - Warning
	Alarms		Mast
	Battery Connector		Oil Leaks
	Belt		Oil Pressure
	Brakes - Parking		Overhead Guard
	Engine Oil Level		Radiator Level
	Forks		Safety Equipment
	Fuel		Steering
	Gauges		Tires
	Horn		Unusual Noises
	Hoses		Other: _____

Notes: _____
_____
_____
_____
_____
_____
_____

Operator's Name	Supervisor's Name
_____	_____
Operator's Signature	Supervisor's Signature
_____	_____

PROPANE FORKLIFT INSPECTION CHECKLIST

Date: _____ Shift: _____

Forklift Serial Number: _____

Hour Meter Start: _____ End: _____ Total Hours: _____

	Gas gauge		Hour Meter
	LPG tank and locator pin		Hydraulic Controls
	LPG tank hose		Lights - Head and Tail
	Accelerator		Lights - Warning
	Alarms		Mast
	Battery Connector		Oil Leaks
	Belt		Oil Pressure
	Brakes - Parking		Overhead Guard
	Engine Oil Level		Radiator Level
	Forks		Safety Equipment
	Fuel		Steering
	Gauges		Tires
	Horn		Unusual Noises
	Hoses		Other: _____

Notes: _____

_____

_____

_____

_____

_____

_____

Operator's Name	Supervisor's Name
_____	_____
Operator's Signature	Supervisor's Signature
_____	_____

PROPANE FORKLIFT INSPECTION CHECKLIST

Date: _____ Shift: _____

Forklift Serial Number: _____

Hour Meter Start: _____ End: _____ Total Hours: _____

	Gas gauge		Hour Meter
	LPG tank and locator pin		Hydraulic Controls
	LPG tank hose		Lights - Head and Tail
	Accelerator		Lights - Warning
	Alarms		Mast
	Battery Connector		Oil Leaks
	Belt		Oil Pressure
	Brakes - Parking		Overhead Guard
	Engine Oil Level		Radiator Level
	Forks		Safety Equipment
	Fuel		Steering
	Gauges		Tires
	Horn		Unusual Noises
	Hoses		Other: _____

Notes: _____
_____
_____
_____
_____
_____

Operator's Name	Supervisor's Name
_____	_____
Operator's Signature	Supervisor's Signature

PROPANE FORKLIFT INSPECTION CHECKLIST

Date: _____ Shift: _____

Forklift Serial Number: _____

Hour Meter Start:_____ End:_____ Total Hours:_____

	Gas gauge		Hour Meter
	LPG tank and locator pin		Hydraulic Controls
	LPG tank hose		Lights - Head and Tail
	Accelerator		Lights - Warning
	Alarms		Mast
	Battery Connector		Oil Leaks
	Belt		Oil Pressure
	Brakes - Parking		Overhead Guard
	Engine Oil Level		Radiator Level
	Forks		Safety Equipment
	Fuel		Steering
	Gauges		Tires
	Horn		Unusual Noises
	Hoses		Other: _____

Notes: _____
_____
_____
_____
_____
_____

Operator's Name	Supervisor's Name
_____	_____
Operator's Signature	Supervisor's Signature
_____	_____

PROPANE FORKLIFT INSPECTION CHECKLIST

Date: _____ Shift: _____

Forklift Serial Number: _____

Hour Meter Start: _____ End: _____ Total Hours: _____

	Gas gauge		Hour Meter
	LPG tank and locator pin		Hydraulic Controls
	LPG tank hose		Lights - Head and Tail
	Accelerator		Lights - Warning
	Alarms		Mast
	Battery Connector		Oil Leaks
	Belt		Oil Pressure
	Brakes - Parking		Overhead Guard
	Engine Oil Level		Radiator Level
	Forks		Safety Equipment
	Fuel		Steering
	Gauges		Tires
	Horn		Unusual Noises
	Hoses		Other: _____

Notes: _____
_____
_____
_____
_____
_____
_____

Operator's Name

_____

Operator's Signature

_____

Supervisor's Name

_____

Supervisor's Signature

_____

PROPANE FORKLIFT INSPECTION CHECKLIST

Date: _____ Shift: _____

Forklift Serial Number: _____

Hour Meter Start: _____ End: _____ Total Hours: _____

	Gas gauge		Hour Meter
	LPG tank and locator pin		Hydraulic Controls
	LPG tank hose		Lights - Head and Tail
	Accelerator		Lights - Warning
	Alarms		Mast
	Battery Connector		Oil Leaks
	Belt		Oil Pressure
	Brakes - Parking		Overhead Guard
	Engine Oil Level		Radiator Level
	Forks		Safety Equipment
	Fuel		Steering
	Gauges		Tires
	Horn		Unusual Noises
	Hoses		Other: _____

Notes: _____

_____

_____

_____

_____

_____

Operator's Name

_____

Operator's Signature

_____

Supervisor's Name

_____

Supervisor's Signature

_____

PROPANE FORKLIFT INSPECTION CHECKLIST

Date: _____ Shift: _____

Forklift Serial Number: _____

Hour Meter Start: _____ End: _____ Total Hours: _____

	Gas gauge		Hour Meter
	LPG tank and locator pin		Hydraulic Controls
	LPG tank hose		Lights - Head and Tail
	Accelerator		Lights - Warning
	Alarms		Mast
	Battery Connector		Oil Leaks
	Belt		Oil Pressure
	Brakes - Parking		Overhead Guard
	Engine Oil Level		Radiator Level
	Forks		Safety Equipment
	Fuel		Steering
	Gauges		Tires
	Horn		Unusual Noises
	Hoses		Other: _____

Notes: _____

_____

_____

_____

_____

_____

Operator's Name	Supervisor's Name
_____	_____
Operator's Signature	Supervisor's Signature
_____	_____

PROPANE FORKLIFT INSPECTION CHECKLIST

Date: _____ Shift: _____

Forklift Serial Number: _____

Hour Meter Start:_____ End:_____ Total Hours:_____

	Gas gauge		Hour Meter
	LPG tank and locator pin		Hydraulic Controls
	LPG tank hose		Lights - Head and Tail
	Accelerator		Lights - Warning
	Alarms		Mast
	Battery Connector		Oil Leaks
	Belt		Oil Pressure
	Brakes - Parking		Overhead Guard
	Engine Oil Level		Radiator Level
	Forks		Safety Equipment
	Fuel		Steering
	Gauges		Tires
	Horn		Unusual Noises
	Hoses		Other: _____

Notes: _____
_____
_____
_____
_____
_____

Operator's Name

_____

Operator's Signature

_____

Supervisor's Name

_____

Supervisor's Signature

_____

PROPANE FORKLIFT INSPECTION CHECKLIST

Date: _____ Shift: _____

Forklift Serial Number: _____

Hour Meter Start: _____ End: _____ Total Hours: _____

	Gas gauge		Hour Meter
	LPG tank and locator pin		Hydraulic Controls
	LPG tank hose		Lights - Head and Tail
	Accelerator		Lights - Warning
	Alarms		Mast
	Battery Connector		Oil Leaks
	Belt		Oil Pressure
	Brakes - Parking		Overhead Guard
	Engine Oil Level		Radiator Level
	Forks		Safety Equipment
	Fuel		Steering
	Gauges		Tires
	Horn		Unusual Noises
	Hoses		Other: _____

Notes: _____
_____
_____
_____
_____
_____

Operator's Name	Supervisor's Name
_____	_____
Operator's Signature	Supervisor's Signature
_____	_____

PROPANE FORKLIFT INSPECTION CHECKLIST

Date: _____ Shift: _____

Forklift Serial Number: _____

Hour Meter Start: _____ End: _____ Total Hours: _____

	Gas gauge		Hour Meter
	LPG tank and locator pin		Hydraulic Controls
	LPG tank hose		Lights - Head and Tail
	Accelerator		Lights - Warning
	Alarms		Mast
	Battery Connector		Oil Leaks
	Belt		Oil Pressure
	Brakes - Parking		Overhead Guard
	Engine Oil Level		Radiator Level
	Forks		Safety Equipment
	Fuel		Steering
	Gauges		Tires
	Horn		Unusual Noises
	Hoses		Other: _____

Notes: _____
_____
_____
_____
_____
_____

Operator's Name	Supervisor's Name
_____	_____
Operator's Signature	Supervisor's Signature
_____	_____

PROPANE FORKLIFT INSPECTION CHECKLIST

Date: _____ Shift: _____

Forklift Serial Number: _____

Hour Meter Start: _____ End: _____ Total Hours: _____

	Gas gauge		Hour Meter
	LPG tank and locator pin		Hydraulic Controls
	LPG tank hose		Lights - Head and Tail
	Accelerator		Lights - Warning
	Alarms		Mast
	Battery Connector		Oil Leaks
	Belt		Oil Pressure
	Brakes - Parking		Overhead Guard
	Engine Oil Level		Radiator Level
	Forks		Safety Equipment
	Fuel		Steering
	Gauges		Tires
	Horn		Unusual Noises
	Hoses		Other: _____

Notes: _____
_____
_____
_____
_____
_____

Operator's Name

_____

Operator's Signature

_____

Supervisor's Name

_____

Supervisor's Signature

_____

PROPANE FORKLIFT INSPECTION CHECKLIST

Date: _____ Shift: _____

Forklift Serial Number: _____

Hour Meter Start: _____ End: _____ Total Hours: _____

	Gas gauge		Hour Meter
	LPG tank and locator pin		Hydraulic Controls
	LPG tank hose		Lights - Head and Tail
	Accelerator		Lights - Warning
	Alarms		Mast
	Battery Connector		Oil Leaks
	Belt		Oil Pressure
	Brakes - Parking		Overhead Guard
	Engine Oil Level		Radiator Level
	Forks		Safety Equipment
	Fuel		Steering
	Gauges		Tires
	Horn		Unusual Noises
	Hoses		Other: _____

Notes: _____
_____
_____
_____
_____
_____
_____

Operator's Name	Supervisor's Name
_____	_____
Operator's Signature	Supervisor's Signature
_____	_____

PROPANE FORKLIFT INSPECTION CHECKLIST

Date: _____ Shift: _____

Forklift Serial Number: _____

Hour Meter Start: _____ End: _____ Total Hours: _____

	Gas gauge		Hour Meter
	LPG tank and locator pin		Hydraulic Controls
	LPG tank hose		Lights - Head and Tail
	Accelerator		Lights - Warning
	Alarms		Mast
	Battery Connector		Oil Leaks
	Belt		Oil Pressure
	Brakes - Parking		Overhead Guard
	Engine Oil Level		Radiator Level
	Forks		Safety Equipment
	Fuel		Steering
	Gauges		Tires
	Horn		Unusual Noises
	Hoses		Other: _____

Notes: _____
_____
_____
_____
_____
_____
_____

Operator's Name

_____

Operator's Signature

_____

Supervisor's Name

_____

Supervisor's Signature

_____

PROPANE FORKLIFT INSPECTION CHECKLIST

Date: _____ Shift: _____

Forklift Serial Number: _____

Hour Meter Start: _____ End: _____ Total Hours: _____

	Gas gauge		Hour Meter
	LPG tank and locator pin		Hydraulic Controls
	LPG tank hose		Lights - Head and Tail
	Accelerator		Lights - Warning
	Alarms		Mast
	Battery Connector		Oil Leaks
	Belt		Oil Pressure
	Brakes - Parking		Overhead Guard
	Engine Oil Level		Radiator Level
	Forks		Safety Equipment
	Fuel		Steering
	Gauges		Tires
	Horn		Unusual Noises
	Hoses		Other: _____

Notes: _____
_____
_____
_____
_____
_____

Operator's Name
_____

Operator's Signature
_____

Supervisor's Name
_____

Supervisor's Signature
_____

PROPANE FORKLIFT INSPECTION CHECKLIST

Date: _____ Shift: _____

Forklift Serial Number: _____

Hour Meter Start: _____ End: _____ Total Hours: _____

	Gas gauge		Hour Meter
	LPG tank and locator pin		Hydraulic Controls
	LPG tank hose		Lights - Head and Tail
	Accelerator		Lights - Warning
	Alarms		Mast
	Battery Connector		Oil Leaks
	Belt		Oil Pressure
	Brakes - Parking		Overhead Guard
	Engine Oil Level		Radiator Level
	Forks		Safety Equipment
	Fuel		Steering
	Gauges		Tires
	Horn		Unusual Noises
	Hoses		Other: _____

Notes: _____
_____
_____
_____
_____
_____

Operator's Name

_____

Operator's Signature

_____

Supervisor's Name

_____

Supervisor's Signature

_____

PROPANE FORKLIFT INSPECTION CHECKLIST

Date: _____ Shift: _____

Forklift Serial Number: _____

Hour Meter Start: _____ End: _____ Total Hours: _____

Gas gauge		Hour Meter	
LPG tank and locator pin		Hydraulic Controls	
LPG tank hose		Lights - Head and Tail	
Accelerator		Lights - Warning	
Alarms		Mast	
Battery Connector		Oil Leaks	
Belt		Oil Pressure	
Brakes - Parking		Overhead Guard	
Engine Oil Level		Radiator Level	
Forks		Safety Equipment	
Fuel		Steering	
Gauges		Tires	
Horn		Unusual Noises	
Hoses		Other: _____	

Notes: _____
_____
_____
_____
_____
_____

Operator's Name	Supervisor's Name
_____	_____
Operator's Signature	Supervisor's Signature
_____	_____

PROPANE FORKLIFT INSPECTION CHECKLIST

Date: _____ Shift: _____

Forklift Serial Number: _____

Hour Meter Start: _____ End: _____ Total Hours: _____

	Gas gauge		Hour Meter
	LPG tank and locator pin		Hydraulic Controls
	LPG tank hose		Lights - Head and Tail
	Accelerator		Lights - Warning
	Alarms		Mast
	Battery Connector		Oil Leaks
	Belt		Oil Pressure
	Brakes - Parking		Overhead Guard
	Engine Oil Level		Radiator Level
	Forks		Safety Equipment
	Fuel		Steering
	Gauges		Tires
	Horn		Unusual Noises
	Hoses		Other: _____

Notes: _____
_____
_____
_____
_____
_____

Operator's Name

_____

Operator's Signature

_____

Supervisor's Name

_____

Supervisor's Signature

_____

PROPANE FORKLIFT INSPECTION CHECKLIST

Date: _____ Shift: _____

Forklift Serial Number: _____

Hour Meter Start: _____ End: _____ Total Hours: _____

	Gas gauge		Hour Meter
	LPG tank and locator pin		Hydraulic Controls
	LPG tank hose		Lights - Head and Tail
	Accelerator		Lights - Warning
	Alarms		Mast
	Battery Connector		Oil Leaks
	Belt		Oil Pressure
	Brakes - Parking		Overhead Guard
	Engine Oil Level		Radiator Level
	Forks		Safety Equipment
	Fuel		Steering
	Gauges		Tires
	Horn		Unusual Noises
	Hoses		Other: _____

Notes: _____
_____
_____
_____
_____
_____

Operator's Name

_____

Operator's Signature

_____

Supervisor's Name

_____

Supervisor's Signature

_____

PROPANE FORKLIFT INSPECTION CHECKLIST

Date: _____ Shift: _____

Forklift Serial Number: _____

Hour Meter Start: _____ End: _____ Total Hours: _____

	Gas gauge		Hour Meter
	LPG tank and locator pin		Hydraulic Controls
	LPG tank hose		Lights - Head and Tail
	Accelerator		Lights - Warning
	Alarms		Mast
	Battery Connector		Oil Leaks
	Belt		Oil Pressure
	Brakes - Parking		Overhead Guard
	Engine Oil Level		Radiator Level
	Forks		Safety Equipment
	Fuel		Steering
	Gauges		Tires
	Horn		Unusual Noises
	Hoses		Other: _____

Notes: _____
_____
_____
_____
_____
_____

Operator's Name
_____

Operator's Signature
_____

Supervisor's Name
_____

Supervisor's Signature
_____

PROPANE FORKLIFT INSPECTION CHECKLIST

Date: _____ Shift: _____

Forklift Serial Number: _____

Hour Meter Start: _____ End: _____ Total Hours: _____

	Gas gauge		Hour Meter
	LPG tank and locator pin		Hydraulic Controls
	LPG tank hose		Lights - Head and Tail
	Accelerator		Lights - Warning
	Alarms		Mast
	Battery Connector		Oil Leaks
	Belt		Oil Pressure
	Brakes - Parking		Overhead Guard
	Engine Oil Level		Radiator Level
	Forks		Safety Equipment
	Fuel		Steering
	Gauges		Tires
	Horn		Unusual Noises
	Hoses		Other: _____

Notes: _____
_____
_____
_____
_____
_____

Operator's Name	Supervisor's Name
_____	_____
Operator's Signature	Supervisor's Signature
_____	_____

PROPANE FORKLIFT INSPECTION CHECKLIST

Date: _____ Shift: _____

Forklift Serial Number: _____

Hour Meter Start: _____ End: _____ Total Hours: _____

Gas gauge	Hour Meter
LPG tank and locator pin	Hydraulic Controls
LPG tank hose	Lights - Head and Tail
Accelerator	Lights - Warning
Alarms	Mast
Battery Connector	Oil Leaks
Belt	Oil Pressure
Brakes - Parking	Overhead Guard
Engine Oil Level	Radiator Level
Forks	Safety Equipment
Fuel	Steering
Gauges	Tires
Horn	Unusual Noises
Hoses	Other: _____

Notes: _____
_____
_____
_____
_____
_____

Operator's Name	Supervisor's Name
_____	_____
Operator's Signature	Supervisor's Signature
_____	_____

PROPANE FORKLIFT INSPECTION CHECKLIST

Date: _____ Shift: _____

Forklift Serial Number: _____

Hour Meter Start: _____ End: _____ Total Hours: _____

	Gas gauge		Hour Meter
	LPG tank and locator pin		Hydraulic Controls
	LPG tank hose		Lights - Head and Tail
	Accelerator		Lights - Warning
	Alarms		Mast
	Battery Connector		Oil Leaks
	Belt		Oil Pressure
	Brakes - Parking		Overhead Guard
	Engine Oil Level		Radiator Level
	Forks		Safety Equipment
	Fuel		Steering
	Gauges		Tires
	Horn		Unusual Noises
	Hoses		Other: _____

Notes: _____
_____
_____
_____
_____
_____

Operator's Name	Supervisor's Name
Operator's Signature	Supervisor's Signature

PROPANE FORKLIFT INSPECTION CHECKLIST

Date: _____ Shift: _____

Forklift Serial Number: _____

Hour Meter Start: _____ End: _____ Total Hours: _____

	Gas gauge		Hour Meter
	LPG tank and locator pin		Hydraulic Controls
	LPG tank hose		Lights - Head and Tail
	Accelerator		Lights - Warning
	Alarms		Mast
	Battery Connector		Oil Leaks
	Belt		Oil Pressure
	Brakes - Parking		Overhead Guard
	Engine Oil Level		Radiator Level
	Forks		Safety Equipment
	Fuel		Steering
	Gauges		Tires
	Horn		Unusual Noises
	Hoses		Other: _____

Notes: _____
_____
_____
_____
_____
_____

Operator's Name	Supervisor's Name
_____	_____
Operator's Signature	Supervisor's Signature
_____	_____

PROPANE FORKLIFT INSPECTION CHECKLIST

Date: _____ Shift: _____

Forklift Serial Number: _____

Hour Meter Start: _____ End: _____ Total Hours: _____

	Gas gauge		Hour Meter
	LPG tank and locator pin		Hydraulic Controls
	LPG tank hose		Lights - Head and Tail
	Accelerator		Lights - Warning
	Alarms		Mast
	Battery Connector		Oil Leaks
	Belt		Oil Pressure
	Brakes - Parking		Overhead Guard
	Engine Oil Level		Radiator Level
	Forks		Safety Equipment
	Fuel		Steering
	Gauges		Tires
	Horn		Unusual Noises
	Hoses		Other: _____

Notes: _____

_____

_____

_____

_____

_____

Operator's Name	Supervisor's Name
_____	_____
Operator's Signature	Supervisor's Signature
_____	_____

PROPANE FORKLIFT INSPECTION CHECKLIST

Date: _____ Shift: _____

Forklift Serial Number: _____

Hour Meter Start: _____ End: _____ Total Hours: _____

	Gas gauge		Hour Meter
	LPG tank and locator pin		Hydraulic Controls
	LPG tank hose		Lights - Head and Tail
	Accelerator		Lights - Warning
	Alarms		Mast
	Battery Connector		Oil Leaks
	Belt		Oil Pressure
	Brakes - Parking		Overhead Guard
	Engine Oil Level		Radiator Level
	Forks		Safety Equipment
	Fuel		Steering
	Gauges		Tires
	Horn		Unusual Noises
	Hoses		Other: _____

Notes: _____

_____

_____

_____

_____

_____

Operator's Name

_____

Operator's Signature

_____

Supervisor's Name

_____

Supervisor's Signature

_____

PROPANE FORKLIFT INSPECTION CHECKLIST

Date: _____ Shift: _____

Forklift Serial Number: _____

Hour Meter Start: _____ End: _____ Total Hours: _____

	Gas gauge		Hour Meter
	LPG tank and locator pin		Hydraulic Controls
	LPG tank hose		Lights - Head and Tail
	Accelerator		Lights - Warning
	Alarms		Mast
	Battery Connector		Oil Leaks
	Belt		Oil Pressure
	Brakes - Parking		Overhead Guard
	Engine Oil Level		Radiator Level
	Forks		Safety Equipment
	Fuel		Steering
	Gauges		Tires
	Horn		Unusual Noises
	Hoses		Other: _____

Notes: _____
_____
_____
_____
_____
_____

Operator's Name

_____

Operator's Signature

_____

Supervisor's Name

_____

Supervisor's Signature

_____

PROPANE FORKLIFT INSPECTION CHECKLIST

Date: _____ Shift: _____

Forklift Serial Number: _____

Hour Meter Start: _____ End: _____ Total Hours: _____

	Gas gauge		Hour Meter
	LPG tank and locator pin		Hydraulic Controls
	LPG tank hose		Lights - Head and Tail
	Accelerator		Lights - Warning
	Alarms		Mast
	Battery Connector		Oil Leaks
	Belt		Oil Pressure
	Brakes - Parking		Overhead Guard
	Engine Oil Level		Radiator Level
	Forks		Safety Equipment
	Fuel		Steering
	Gauges		Tires
	Horn		Unusual Noises
	Hoses		Other: _____

Notes: _____

_____

_____

_____

_____

_____

Operator's Name

_____

Operator's Signature

_____

Supervisor's Name

_____

Supervisor's Signature

_____

PROPANE FORKLIFT INSPECTION CHECKLIST

Date: _____ Shift: _____

Forklift Serial Number: _____

Hour Meter Start: _____ End: _____ Total Hours: _____

	Gas gauge		Hour Meter
	LPG tank and locator pin		Hydraulic Controls
	LPG tank hose		Lights - Head and Tail
	Accelerator		Lights - Warning
	Alarms		Mast
	Battery Connector		Oil Leaks
	Belt		Oil Pressure
	Brakes - Parking		Overhead Guard
	Engine Oil Level		Radiator Level
	Forks		Safety Equipment
	Fuel		Steering
	Gauges		Tires
	Horn		Unusual Noises
	Hoses		Other: _____

Notes: _____
_____
_____
_____
_____
_____

Operator's Name	Supervisor's Name
_____	_____
Operator's Signature	Supervisor's Signature
_____	_____

PROPANE FORKLIFT INSPECTION CHECKLIST

Date: _____ Shift: _____

Forklift Serial Number: _____

Hour Meter Start: _____ End: _____ Total Hours: _____

Gas gauge	Hour Meter
LPG tank and locator pin	Hydraulic Controls
LPG tank hose	Lights - Head and Tail
Accelerator	Lights - Warning
Alarms	Mast
Battery Connector	Oil Leaks
Belt	Oil Pressure
Brakes - Parking	Overhead Guard
Engine Oil Level	Radiator Level
Forks	Safety Equipment
Fuel	Steering
Gauges	Tires
Horn	Unusual Noises
Hoses	Other: _____

Notes: _____
_____
_____
_____
_____
_____

Operator's Name	Supervisor's Name
Operator's Signature	Supervisor's Signature

PROPANE FORKLIFT INSPECTION CHECKLIST

Date: _____ Shift: _____

Forklift Serial Number: _____

Hour Meter Start: _____ End: _____ Total Hours: _____

	Gas gauge		Hour Meter
	LPG tank and locator pin		Hydraulic Controls
	LPG tank hose		Lights - Head and Tail
	Accelerator		Lights - Warning
	Alarms		Mast
	Battery Connector		Oil Leaks
	Belt		Oil Pressure
	Brakes - Parking		Overhead Guard
	Engine Oil Level		Radiator Level
	Forks		Safety Equipment
	Fuel		Steering
	Gauges		Tires
	Horn		Unusual Noises
	Hoses		Other: _____

Notes: _____
_____
_____
_____
_____
_____

Operator's Name	Supervisor's Name
_____	_____
Operator's Signature	Supervisor's Signature
_____	_____

PROPANE FORKLIFT INSPECTION CHECKLIST

Date: _____ Shift: _____

Forklift Serial Number: _____

Hour Meter Start: _____ End: _____ Total Hours: _____

	Gas gauge		Hour Meter
	LPG tank and locator pin		Hydraulic Controls
	LPG tank hose		Lights - Head and Tail
	Accelerator		Lights - Warning
	Alarms		Mast
	Battery Connector		Oil Leaks
	Belt		Oil Pressure
	Brakes - Parking		Overhead Guard
	Engine Oil Level		Radiator Level
	Forks		Safety Equipment
	Fuel		Steering
	Gauges		Tires
	Horn		Unusual Noises
	Hoses		Other: _____

Notes: _____
_____
_____
_____
_____
_____

Operator's Name	Supervisor's Name
_____	_____
Operator's Signature	Supervisor's Signature
_____	_____

PROPANE FORKLIFT INSPECTION CHECKLIST

Date: _____ Shift: _____

Forklift Serial Number: _____

Hour Meter Start: _____ End: _____ Total Hours: _____

	Gas gauge		Hour Meter
	LPG tank and locator pin		Hydraulic Controls
	LPG tank hose		Lights - Head and Tail
	Accelerator		Lights - Warning
	Alarms		Mast
	Battery Connector		Oil Leaks
	Belt		Oil Pressure
	Brakes - Parking		Overhead Guard
	Engine Oil Level		Radiator Level
	Forks		Safety Equipment
	Fuel		Steering
	Gauges		Tires
	Horn		Unusual Noises
	Hoses		Other: _____

Notes: _____

_____

_____

_____

_____

_____

Operator's Name	Supervisor's Name
_____	_____
Operator's Signature	Supervisor's Signature
_____	_____

PROPANE FORKLIFT INSPECTION CHECKLIST

Date: _____ Shift: _____

Forklift Serial Number: _____

Hour Meter Start: _____ End: _____ Total Hours: _____

	Gas gauge		Hour Meter
	LPG tank and locator pin		Hydraulic Controls
	LPG tank hose		Lights - Head and Tail
	Accelerator		Lights - Warning
	Alarms		Mast
	Battery Connector		Oil Leaks
	Belt		Oil Pressure
	Brakes - Parking		Overhead Guard
	Engine Oil Level		Radiator Level
	Forks		Safety Equipment
	Fuel		Steering
	Gauges		Tires
	Horn		Unusual Noises
	Hoses		Other: _____

Notes: _____

_____

_____

_____

_____

_____

Operator's Name	Supervisor's Name
_____	_____
Operator's Signature	Supervisor's Signature
_____	_____

PROPANE FORKLIFT INSPECTION CHECKLIST

Date: _____ Shift: _____

Forklift Serial Number: _____

Hour Meter Start: _____ End: _____ Total Hours: _____

	Gas gauge		Hour Meter
	LPG tank and locator pin		Hydraulic Controls
	LPG tank hose		Lights - Head and Tail
	Accelerator		Lights - Warning
	Alarms		Mast
	Battery Connector		Oil Leaks
	Belt		Oil Pressure
	Brakes - Parking		Overhead Guard
	Engine Oil Level		Radiator Level
	Forks		Safety Equipment
	Fuel		Steering
	Gauges		Tires
	Horn		Unusual Noises
	Hoses		Other: _____

Notes: _____

_____

_____

_____

_____

_____

Operator's Name	Supervisor's Name
_____	_____
Operator's Signature	Supervisor's Signature
_____	_____

PROPANE FORKLIFT INSPECTION CHECKLIST

Date: _____ Shift: _____

Forklift Serial Number: _____

Hour Meter Start: _____ End: _____ Total Hours: _____

	Gas gauge		Hour Meter
	LPG tank and locator pin		Hydraulic Controls
	LPG tank hose		Lights - Head and Tail
	Accelerator		Lights - Warning
	Alarms		Mast
	Battery Connector		Oil Leaks
	Belt		Oil Pressure
	Brakes - Parking		Overhead Guard
	Engine Oil Level		Radiator Level
	Forks		Safety Equipment
	Fuel		Steering
	Gauges		Tires
	Horn		Unusual Noises
	Hoses		Other: _____

Notes: _____
_____
_____
_____
_____
_____

Operator's Name

_____

Operator's Signature

_____

Supervisor's Name

_____

Supervisor's Signature

_____

PROPANE FORKLIFT INSPECTION CHECKLIST

Date: _____ Shift: _____

Forklift Serial Number: _____

Hour Meter Start: _____ End: _____ Total Hours: _____

	Gas gauge		Hour Meter
	LPG tank and locator pin		Hydraulic Controls
	LPG tank hose		Lights - Head and Tail
	Accelerator		Lights - Warning
	Alarms		Mast
	Battery Connector		Oil Leaks
	Belt		Oil Pressure
	Brakes - Parking		Overhead Guard
	Engine Oil Level		Radiator Level
	Forks		Safety Equipment
	Fuel		Steering
	Gauges		Tires
	Horn		Unusual Noises
	Hoses		Other: _____

Notes: _____
_____
_____
_____
_____
_____

Operator's Name	Supervisor's Name
_____	_____
Operator's Signature	Supervisor's Signature
_____	_____

PROPANE FORKLIFT INSPECTION CHECKLIST

Date: _____ Shift: _____

Forklift Serial Number: _____

Hour Meter Start: _____ End: _____ Total Hours: _____

	Gas gauge		Hour Meter
	LPG tank and locator pin		Hydraulic Controls
	LPG tank hose		Lights - Head and Tail
	Accelerator		Lights - Warning
	Alarms		Mast
	Battery Connector		Oil Leaks
	Belt		Oil Pressure
	Brakes - Parking		Overhead Guard
	Engine Oil Level		Radiator Level
	Forks		Safety Equipment
	Fuel		Steering
	Gauges		Tires
	Horn		Unusual Noises
	Hoses		Other: _____

Notes: _____
_____
_____
_____
_____
_____
_____

Operator's Name	Supervisor's Name
_____	_____
Operator's Signature	Supervisor's Signature
_____	_____

PROPANE FORKLIFT INSPECTION CHECKLIST

Date: _____ Shift: _____

Forklift Serial Number: _____

Hour Meter Start: _____ End: _____ Total Hours: _____

	Gas gauge		Hour Meter
	LPG tank and locator pin		Hydraulic Controls
	LPG tank hose		Lights - Head and Tail
	Accelerator		Lights - Warning
	Alarms		Mast
	Battery Connector		Oil Leaks
	Belt		Oil Pressure
	Brakes - Parking		Overhead Guard
	Engine Oil Level		Radiator Level
	Forks		Safety Equipment
	Fuel		Steering
	Gauges		Tires
	Horn		Unusual Noises
	Hoses		Other: _____

Notes: _____
_____
_____
_____
_____
_____

Operator's Name	Supervisor's Name
_____	_____
Operator's Signature	Supervisor's Signature
_____	_____

PROPANE FORKLIFT INSPECTION CHECKLIST

Date: _____ Shift: _____

Forklift Serial Number: _____

Hour Meter Start: _____ End: _____ Total Hours: _____

	Gas gauge		Hour Meter
	LPG tank and locator pin		Hydraulic Controls
	LPG tank hose		Lights - Head and Tail
	Accelerator		Lights - Warning
	Alarms		Mast
	Battery Connector		Oil Leaks
	Belt		Oil Pressure
	Brakes - Parking		Overhead Guard
	Engine Oil Level		Radiator Level
	Forks		Safety Equipment
	Fuel		Steering
	Gauges		Tires
	Horn		Unusual Noises
	Hoses		Other: _____

Notes: _____
_____
_____
_____
_____
_____

Operator's Name	Supervisor's Name
_____	_____
Operator's Signature	Supervisor's Signature
_____	_____

PROPANE FORKLIFT INSPECTION CHECKLIST

Date: _____ Shift: _____

Forklift Serial Number: _____

Hour Meter Start: _____ End: _____ Total Hours: _____

Gas gauge		Hour Meter	
LPG tank and locator pin		Hydraulic Controls	
LPG tank hose		Lights - Head and Tail	
Accelerator		Lights - Warning	
Alarms		Mast	
Battery Connector		Oil Leaks	
Belt		Oil Pressure	
Brakes - Parking		Overhead Guard	
Engine Oil Level		Radiator Level	
Forks		Safety Equipment	
Fuel		Steering	
Gauges		Tires	
Horn		Unusual Noises	
Hoses		Other: _____	

Notes: _____
_____
_____
_____
_____
_____

Operator's Name	Supervisor's Name
_____	_____
Operator's Signature	Supervisor's Signature
_____	_____

PROPANE FORKLIFT INSPECTION CHECKLIST

Date: _____ Shift: _____

Forklift Serial Number: _____

Hour Meter Start: _____ End: _____ Total Hours: _____

Gas gauge	Hour Meter
LPG tank and locator pin	Hydraulic Controls
LPG tank hose	Lights - Head and Tail
Accelerator	Lights - Warning
Alarms	Mast
Battery Connector	Oil Leaks
Belt	Oil Pressure
Brakes - Parking	Overhead Guard
Engine Oil Level	Radiator Level
Forks	Safety Equipment
Fuel	Steering
Gauges	Tires
Horn	Unusual Noises
Hoses	Other: _____

Notes: _____
_____
_____
_____
_____
_____

Operator's Name	Supervisor's Name
_____	_____
Operator's Signature	Supervisor's Signature
_____	_____

PROPANE FORKLIFT INSPECTION CHECKLIST

Date: _____ Shift: _____

Forklift Serial Number: _____

Hour Meter Start: _____ End: _____ Total Hours: _____

	Gas gauge		Hour Meter
	LPG tank and locator pin		Hydraulic Controls
	LPG tank hose		Lights - Head and Tail
	Accelerator		Lights - Warning
	Alarms		Mast
	Battery Connector		Oil Leaks
	Belt		Oil Pressure
	Brakes - Parking		Overhead Guard
	Engine Oil Level		Radiator Level
	Forks		Safety Equipment
	Fuel		Steering
	Gauges		Tires
	Horn		Unusual Noises
	Hoses		Other: _____

Notes: _____
_____
_____
_____
_____
_____

Operator's Name	Supervisor's Name
_____	_____
Operator's Signature	Supervisor's Signature
_____	_____

PROPANE FORKLIFT INSPECTION CHECKLIST

Date: _____ Shift: _____

Forklift Serial Number: _____

Hour Meter Start: _____ End: _____ Total Hours: _____

	Gas gauge		Hour Meter
	LPG tank and locator pin		Hydraulic Controls
	LPG tank hose		Lights - Head and Tail
	Accelerator		Lights - Warning
	Alarms		Mast
	Battery Connector		Oil Leaks
	Belt		Oil Pressure
	Brakes - Parking		Overhead Guard
	Engine Oil Level		Radiator Level
	Forks		Safety Equipment
	Fuel		Steering
	Gauges		Tires
	Horn		Unusual Noises
	Hoses		Other: _____

Notes: _____
_____
_____
_____
_____
_____
_____

Operator's Name	Supervisor's Name
_____	_____
Operator's Signature	Supervisor's Signature
_____	_____

PROPANE FORKLIFT INSPECTION CHECKLIST

Date: _____ Shift: _____

Forklift Serial Number: _____

Hour Meter Start: _____ End: _____ Total Hours: _____

	Gas gauge		Hour Meter
	LPG tank and locator pin		Hydraulic Controls
	LPG tank hose		Lights - Head and Tail
	Accelerator		Lights - Warning
	Alarms		Mast
	Battery Connector		Oil Leaks
	Belt		Oil Pressure
	Brakes - Parking		Overhead Guard
	Engine Oil Level		Radiator Level
	Forks		Safety Equipment
	Fuel		Steering
	Gauges		Tires
	Horn		Unusual Noises
	Hoses		Other: _____

Notes: _____
_____
_____
_____
_____
_____

Operator's Name	Supervisor's Name
_____	_____
Operator's Signature	Supervisor's Signature
_____	_____

PROPANE FORKLIFT INSPECTION CHECKLIST

Date: _____ Shift: _____

Forklift Serial Number: _____

Hour Meter Start: _____ End: _____ Total Hours: _____

	Gas gauge		Hour Meter
	LPG tank and locator pin		Hydraulic Controls
	LPG tank hose		Lights - Head and Tail
	Accelerator		Lights - Warning
	Alarms		Mast
	Battery Connector		Oil Leaks
	Belt		Oil Pressure
	Brakes - Parking		Overhead Guard
	Engine Oil Level		Radiator Level
	Forks		Safety Equipment
	Fuel		Steering
	Gauges		Tires
	Horn		Unusual Noises
	Hoses		Other: _____

Notes: _____
_____
_____
_____
_____
_____

Operator's Name	Supervisor's Name
_____	_____
Operator's Signature	Supervisor's Signature
_____	_____

PROPANE FORKLIFT INSPECTION CHECKLIST

Date: _____ Shift: _____

Forklift Serial Number: _____

Hour Meter Start: _____ End: _____ Total Hours: _____

	Gas gauge		Hour Meter
	LPG tank and locator pin		Hydraulic Controls
	LPG tank hose		Lights - Head and Tail
	Accelerator		Lights - Warning
	Alarms		Mast
	Battery Connector		Oil Leaks
	Belt		Oil Pressure
	Brakes - Parking		Overhead Guard
	Engine Oil Level		Radiator Level
	Forks		Safety Equipment
	Fuel		Steering
	Gauges		Tires
	Horn		Unusual Noises
	Hoses		Other: _____

Notes: _____
_____
_____
_____
_____
_____

Operator's Name	Supervisor's Name
_____	_____
Operator's Signature	Supervisor's Signature
_____	_____

PROPANE FORKLIFT INSPECTION CHECKLIST

Date: _____ Shift: _____

Forklift Serial Number: _____

Hour Meter Start: _____ End: _____ Total Hours: _____

	Gas gauge		Hour Meter
	LPG tank and locator pin		Hydraulic Controls
	LPG tank hose		Lights - Head and Tail
	Accelerator		Lights - Warning
	Alarms		Mast
	Battery Connector		Oil Leaks
	Belt		Oil Pressure
	Brakes - Parking		Overhead Guard
	Engine Oil Level		Radiator Level
	Forks		Safety Equipment
	Fuel		Steering
	Gauges		Tires
	Horn		Unusual Noises
	Hoses		Other: _____

Notes: _____
_____
_____
_____
_____
_____

Operator's Name	Supervisor's Name
_____	_____
Operator's Signature	Supervisor's Signature
_____	_____

PROPANE FORKLIFT INSPECTION CHECKLIST

Date: _____ Shift: _____

Forklift Serial Number: _____

Hour Meter Start: _____ End: _____ Total Hours: _____

	Gas gauge		Hour Meter
	LPG tank and locator pin		Hydraulic Controls
	LPG tank hose		Lights - Head and Tail
	Accelerator		Lights - Warning
	Alarms		Mast
	Battery Connector		Oil Leaks
	Belt		Oil Pressure
	Brakes - Parking		Overhead Guard
	Engine Oil Level		Radiator Level
	Forks		Safety Equipment
	Fuel		Steering
	Gauges		Tires
	Horn		Unusual Noises
	Hoses		Other: _____

Notes: _____
_____
_____
_____
_____
_____

Operator's Name	Supervisor's Name
_____	_____
Operator's Signature	Supervisor's Signature
_____	_____

PROPANE FORKLIFT INSPECTION CHECKLIST

Date: _____ Shift: _____

Forklift Serial Number: _____

Hour Meter Start: _____ End: _____ Total Hours: _____

	Gas gauge		Hour Meter
	LPG tank and locator pin		Hydraulic Controls
	LPG tank hose		Lights - Head and Tail
	Accelerator		Lights - Warning
	Alarms		Mast
	Battery Connector		Oil Leaks
	Belt		Oil Pressure
	Brakes - Parking		Overhead Guard
	Engine Oil Level		Radiator Level
	Forks		Safety Equipment
	Fuel		Steering
	Gauges		Tires
	Horn		Unusual Noises
	Hoses		Other: _____

Notes: _____
_____
_____
_____
_____
_____

Operator's Name

_____

Operator's Signature

_____

Supervisor's Name

_____

Supervisor's Signature

_____

PROPANE FORKLIFT INSPECTION CHECKLIST

Date: _____ Shift: _____

Forklift Serial Number: _____

Hour Meter Start: _____ End: _____ Total Hours: _____

	Gas gauge		Hour Meter
	LPG tank and locator pin		Hydraulic Controls
	LPG tank hose		Lights - Head and Tail
	Accelerator		Lights - Warning
	Alarms		Mast
	Battery Connector		Oil Leaks
	Belt		Oil Pressure
	Brakes - Parking		Overhead Guard
	Engine Oil Level		Radiator Level
	Forks		Safety Equipment
	Fuel		Steering
	Gauges		Tires
	Horn		Unusual Noises
	Hoses		Other: _____

Notes: _____
_____
_____
_____
_____
_____

Operator's Name	Supervisor's Name
_____	_____
Operator's Signature	Supervisor's Signature
_____	_____

PROPANE FORKLIFT INSPECTION CHECKLIST

Date: _____ Shift: _____

Forklift Serial Number: _____

Hour Meter Start: _____ End: _____ Total Hours: _____

Gas gauge		Hour Meter	
LPG tank and locator pin		Hydraulic Controls	
LPG tank hose		Lights - Head and Tail	
Accelerator		Lights - Warning	
Alarms		Mast	
Battery Connector		Oil Leaks	
Belt		Oil Pressure	
Brakes - Parking		Overhead Guard	
Engine Oil Level		Radiator Level	
Forks		Safety Equipment	
Fuel		Steering	
Gauges		Tires	
Horn		Unusual Noises	
Hoses		Other: _____	

Notes: _____
_____
_____
_____
_____
_____

Operator's Name	Supervisor's Name
_____	_____
Operator's Signature	Supervisor's Signature
_____	_____

PROPANE FORKLIFT INSPECTION CHECKLIST

Date: _____ Shift: _____

Forklift Serial Number: _____

Hour Meter Start: _____ End: _____ Total Hours: _____

	Gas gauge		Hour Meter
	LPG tank and locator pin		Hydraulic Controls
	LPG tank hose		Lights - Head and Tail
	Accelerator		Lights - Warning
	Alarms		Mast
	Battery Connector		Oil Leaks
	Belt		Oil Pressure
	Brakes - Parking		Overhead Guard
	Engine Oil Level		Radiator Level
	Forks		Safety Equipment
	Fuel		Steering
	Gauges		Tires
	Horn		Unusual Noises
	Hoses		Other: _____

Notes: _____
_____
_____
_____
_____
_____
_____

Operator's Name

_____

Operator's Signature

_____

Supervisor's Name

_____

Supervisor's Signature

_____

PROPANE FORKLIFT INSPECTION CHECKLIST

Date: _____ Shift: _____

Forklift Serial Number: _____

Hour Meter Start: _____ End: _____ Total Hours: _____

	Gas gauge		Hour Meter
	LPG tank and locator pin		Hydraulic Controls
	LPG tank hose		Lights - Head and Tail
	Accelerator		Lights - Warning
	Alarms		Mast
	Battery Connector		Oil Leaks
	Belt		Oil Pressure
	Brakes - Parking		Overhead Guard
	Engine Oil Level		Radiator Level
	Forks		Safety Equipment
	Fuel		Steering
	Gauges		Tires
	Horn		Unusual Noises
	Hoses		Other: _____

Notes: _____
_____
_____
_____
_____
_____

Operator's Name

_____

Operator's Signature

_____

Supervisor's Name

_____

Supervisor's Signature

_____

PROPANE FORKLIFT INSPECTION CHECKLIST

Date: _____ Shift: _____

Forklift Serial Number: _____

Hour Meter Start: _____ End: _____ Total Hours: _____

Gas gauge	Hour Meter
LPG tank and locator pin	Hydraulic Controls
LPG tank hose	Lights - Head and Tail
Accelerator	Lights - Warning
Alarms	Mast
Battery Connector	Oil Leaks
Belt	Oil Pressure
Brakes - Parking	Overhead Guard
Engine Oil Level	Radiator Level
Forks	Safety Equipment
Fuel	Steering
Gauges	Tires
Horn	Unusual Noises
Hoses	Other: _____

Notes: _____
_____
_____
_____
_____
_____

Operator's Name

_____

Operator's Signature

_____

Supervisor's Name

_____

Supervisor's Signature

_____

PROPANE FORKLIFT INSPECTION CHECKLIST

Date: _____ Shift: _____

Forklift Serial Number: _____

Hour Meter Start:_____ End:_____ Total Hours:_____

	Gas gauge		Hour Meter
	LPG tank and locator pin		Hydraulic Controls
	LPG tank hose		Lights - Head and Tail
	Accelerator		Lights - Warning
	Alarms		Mast
	Battery Connector		Oil Leaks
	Belt		Oil Pressure
	Brakes - Parking		Overhead Guard
	Engine Oil Level		Radiator Level
	Forks		Safety Equipment
	Fuel		Steering
	Gauges		Tires
	Horn		Unusual Noises
	Hoses		Other: _____

Notes: _____
_____
_____
_____
_____
_____

Operator's Name	Supervisor's Name
_____	_____
Operator's Signature	Supervisor's Signature
_____	_____

PROPANE FORKLIFT INSPECTION CHECKLIST

Date: _____ Shift: _____

Forklift Serial Number: _____

Hour Meter Start: _____ End: _____ Total Hours: _____

	Gas gauge		Hour Meter
	LPG tank and locator pin		Hydraulic Controls
	LPG tank hose		Lights - Head and Tail
	Accelerator		Lights - Warning
	Alarms		Mast
	Battery Connector		Oil Leaks
	Belt		Oil Pressure
	Brakes - Parking		Overhead Guard
	Engine Oil Level		Radiator Level
	Forks		Safety Equipment
	Fuel		Steering
	Gauges		Tires
	Horn		Unusual Noises
	Hoses		Other: _____

Notes: _____
_____
_____
_____
_____
_____

Operator's Name
_____

Operator's Signature
_____

Supervisor's Name
_____

Supervisor's Signature
_____

PROPANE FORKLIFT INSPECTION CHECKLIST

Date: _____ Shift: _____

Forklift Serial Number: _____

Hour Meter Start: _____ End: _____ Total Hours: _____

Gas gauge	Hour Meter
LPG tank and locator pin	Hydraulic Controls
LPG tank hose	Lights - Head and Tail
Accelerator	Lights - Warning
Alarms	Mast
Battery Connector	Oil Leaks
Belt	Oil Pressure
Brakes - Parking	Overhead Guard
Engine Oil Level	Radiator Level
Forks	Safety Equipment
Fuel	Steering
Gauges	Tires
Horn	Unusual Noises
Hoses	Other: _____

Notes: _____
_____
_____
_____
_____
_____

Operator's Name	Supervisor's Name
_____	_____
Operator's Signature	Supervisor's Signature
_____	_____

PROPANE FORKLIFT INSPECTION CHECKLIST

Date: _____ Shift: _____

Forklift Serial Number: _____

Hour Meter Start: _____ End: _____ Total Hours: _____

	Gas gauge		Hour Meter
	LPG tank and locator pin		Hydraulic Controls
	LPG tank hose		Lights - Head and Tail
	Accelerator		Lights - Warning
	Alarms		Mast
	Battery Connector		Oil Leaks
	Belt		Oil Pressure
	Brakes - Parking		Overhead Guard
	Engine Oil Level		Radiator Level
	Forks		Safety Equipment
	Fuel		Steering
	Gauges		Tires
	Horn		Unusual Noises
	Hoses		Other: _____

Notes: _____
_____
_____
_____
_____
_____
_____

Operator's Name

_____

Operator's Signature

_____

Supervisor's Name

_____

Supervisor's Signature

_____

PROPANE FORKLIFT INSPECTION CHECKLIST

Date: _____ Shift: _____

Forklift Serial Number: _____

Hour Meter Start: _____ End: _____ Total Hours: _____

	Gas gauge		Hour Meter
	LPG tank and locator pin		Hydraulic Controls
	LPG tank hose		Lights - Head and Tail
	Accelerator		Lights - Warning
	Alarms		Mast
	Battery Connector		Oil Leaks
	Belt		Oil Pressure
	Brakes - Parking		Overhead Guard
	Engine Oil Level		Radiator Level
	Forks		Safety Equipment
	Fuel		Steering
	Gauges		Tires
	Horn		Unusual Noises
	Hoses		Other: _____

Notes: _____
_____
_____
_____
_____
_____
_____

Operator's Name

_____

Operator's Signature

_____

Supervisor's Name

_____

Supervisor's Signature

_____

PROPANE FORKLIFT INSPECTION CHECKLIST

Date: _____ Shift: _____

Forklift Serial Number: _____

Hour Meter Start: _____ End: _____ Total Hours: _____

	Gas gauge		Hour Meter
	LPG tank and locator pin		Hydraulic Controls
	LPG tank hose		Lights - Head and Tail
	Accelerator		Lights - Warning
	Alarms		Mast
	Battery Connector		Oil Leaks
	Belt		Oil Pressure
	Brakes - Parking		Overhead Guard
	Engine Oil Level		Radiator Level
	Forks		Safety Equipment
	Fuel		Steering
	Gauges		Tires
	Horn		Unusual Noises
	Hoses		Other: _____

Notes: _____
_____
_____
_____
_____
_____

Operator's Name

_____

Operator's Signature

_____

Supervisor's Name

_____

Supervisor's Signature

_____

PROPANE FORKLIFT INSPECTION CHECKLIST

Date: _____ Shift: _____

Forklift Serial Number: _____

Hour Meter Start: _____ End: _____ Total Hours: _____

	Gas gauge		Hour Meter
	LPG tank and locator pin		Hydraulic Controls
	LPG tank hose		Lights - Head and Tail
	Accelerator		Lights - Warning
	Alarms		Mast
	Battery Connector		Oil Leaks
	Belt		Oil Pressure
	Brakes - Parking		Overhead Guard
	Engine Oil Level		Radiator Level
	Forks		Safety Equipment
	Fuel		Steering
	Gauges		Tires
	Horn		Unusual Noises
	Hoses		Other: _____

Notes: _____
_____
_____
_____
_____
_____

Operator's Name	Supervisor's Name
_____	_____
Operator's Signature	Supervisor's Signature
_____	_____

PROPANE FORKLIFT INSPECTION CHECKLIST

Date: _____ Shift: _____

Forklift Serial Number: _____

Hour Meter Start: _____ End: _____ Total Hours: _____

	Gas gauge		Hour Meter
	LPG tank and locator pin		Hydraulic Controls
	LPG tank hose		Lights - Head and Tail
	Accelerator		Lights - Warning
	Alarms		Mast
	Battery Connector		Oil Leaks
	Belt		Oil Pressure
	Brakes - Parking		Overhead Guard
	Engine Oil Level		Radiator Level
	Forks		Safety Equipment
	Fuel		Steering
	Gauges		Tires
	Horn		Unusual Noises
	Hoses		Other: _____

Notes: _____
_____
_____
_____
_____
_____
_____

Operator's Name	Supervisor's Name
_____	_____
Operator's Signature	Supervisor's Signature
_____	_____

PROPANE FORKLIFT INSPECTION CHECKLIST

Date: _____ Shift: _____

Forklift Serial Number: _____

Hour Meter Start: _____ End: _____ Total Hours: _____

	Gas gauge		Hour Meter
	LPG tank and locator pin		Hydraulic Controls
	LPG tank hose		Lights - Head and Tail
	Accelerator		Lights - Warning
	Alarms		Mast
	Battery Connector		Oil Leaks
	Belt		Oil Pressure
	Brakes - Parking		Overhead Guard
	Engine Oil Level		Radiator Level
	Forks		Safety Equipment
	Fuel		Steering
	Gauges		Tires
	Horn		Unusual Noises
	Hoses		Other: _____

Notes: _____
_____
_____
_____
_____
_____

Operator's Name	Supervisor's Name
Operator's Signature	Supervisor's Signature

PROPANE FORKLIFT INSPECTION CHECKLIST

Date: _____ Shift: _____

Forklift Serial Number: _____

Hour Meter Start: _____ End: _____ Total Hours: _____

	Gas gauge		Hour Meter
	LPG tank and locator pin		Hydraulic Controls
	LPG tank hose		Lights - Head and Tail
	Accelerator		Lights - Warning
	Alarms		Mast
	Battery Connector		Oil Leaks
	Belt		Oil Pressure
	Brakes - Parking		Overhead Guard
	Engine Oil Level		Radiator Level
	Forks		Safety Equipment
	Fuel		Steering
	Gauges		Tires
	Horn		Unusual Noises
	Hoses		Other: _____

Notes: _____
_____
_____
_____
_____
_____

Operator's Name	Supervisor's Name
_____	_____
Operator's Signature	Supervisor's Signature
_____	_____

PROPANE FORKLIFT INSPECTION CHECKLIST

Date: _____ Shift: _____

Forklift Serial Number: _____

Hour Meter Start: _____ End: _____ Total Hours: _____

Gas gauge		Hour Meter
LPG tank and locator pin		Hydraulic Controls
LPG tank hose		Lights - Head and Tail
Accelerator		Lights - Warning
Alarms		Mast
Battery Connector		Oil Leaks
Belt		Oil Pressure
Brakes - Parking		Overhead Guard
Engine Oil Level		Radiator Level
Forks		Safety Equipment
Fuel		Steering
Gauges		Tires
Horn		Unusual Noises
Hoses		Other: _____

Notes: _____
_____
_____
_____
_____
_____

Operator's Name

_____

Operator's Signature

_____

Supervisor's Name

_____

Supervisor's Signature

_____

PROPANE FORKLIFT INSPECTION CHECKLIST

Date: _____ Shift: _____

Forklift Serial Number: _____

Hour Meter Start: _____ End: _____ Total Hours: _____

	Gas gauge		Hour Meter
	LPG tank and locator pin		Hydraulic Controls
	LPG tank hose		Lights - Head and Tail
	Accelerator		Lights - Warning
	Alarms		Mast
	Battery Connector		Oil Leaks
	Belt		Oil Pressure
	Brakes - Parking		Overhead Guard
	Engine Oil Level		Radiator Level
	Forks		Safety Equipment
	Fuel		Steering
	Gauges		Tires
	Horn		Unusual Noises
	Hoses		Other: _____

Notes: _____
_____
_____
_____
_____
_____

Operator's Name	Supervisor's Name
_____	_____
Operator's Signature	Supervisor's Signature
_____	_____

PROPANE FORKLIFT INSPECTION CHECKLIST

Date: _____ Shift: _____

Forklift Serial Number: _____

Hour Meter Start: _____ End: _____ Total Hours: _____

	Gas gauge		Hour Meter
	LPG tank and locator pin		Hydraulic Controls
	LPG tank hose		Lights - Head and Tail
	Accelerator		Lights - Warning
	Alarms		Mast
	Battery Connector		Oil Leaks
	Belt		Oil Pressure
	Brakes - Parking		Overhead Guard
	Engine Oil Level		Radiator Level
	Forks		Safety Equipment
	Fuel		Steering
	Gauges		Tires
	Horn		Unusual Noises
	Hoses		Other: _____

Notes: _____
_____
_____
_____
_____
_____

Operator's Name

_____

Operator's Signature

_____

Supervisor's Name

_____

Supervisor's Signature

_____

PROPANE FORKLIFT INSPECTION CHECKLIST

Date: _____ Shift: _____

Forklift Serial Number: _____

Hour Meter Start: _____ End: _____ Total Hours: _____

	Gas gauge		Hour Meter
	LPG tank and locator pin		Hydraulic Controls
	LPG tank hose		Lights - Head and Tail
	Accelerator		Lights - Warning
	Alarms		Mast
	Battery Connector		Oil Leaks
	Belt		Oil Pressure
	Brakes - Parking		Overhead Guard
	Engine Oil Level		Radiator Level
	Forks		Safety Equipment
	Fuel		Steering
	Gauges		Tires
	Horn		Unusual Noises
	Hoses		Other: _____

Notes: _____
_____
_____
_____
_____
_____

Operator's Name	Supervisor's Name
_____	_____
Operator's Signature	Supervisor's Signature
_____	_____

PROPANE FORKLIFT INSPECTION CHECKLIST

Date: _____ Shift: _____

Forklift Serial Number: _____

Hour Meter Start: _____ End: _____ Total Hours: _____

	Gas gauge		Hour Meter
	LPG tank and locator pin		Hydraulic Controls
	LPG tank hose		Lights - Head and Tail
	Accelerator		Lights - Warning
	Alarms		Mast
	Battery Connector		Oil Leaks
	Belt		Oil Pressure
	Brakes - Parking		Overhead Guard
	Engine Oil Level		Radiator Level
	Forks		Safety Equipment
	Fuel		Steering
	Gauges		Tires
	Horn		Unusual Noises
	Hoses		Other: _____

Notes: _____
_____
_____
_____
_____
_____

Operator's Name	Supervisor's Name
Operator's Signature	Supervisor's Signature

PROPANE FORKLIFT INSPECTION CHECKLIST

Date: _____ Shift: _____

Forklift Serial Number: _____

Hour Meter Start: _____ End: _____ Total Hours: _____

	Gas gauge			Hour Meter
	LPG tank and locator pin			Hydraulic Controls
	LPG tank hose			Lights - Head and Tail
	Accelerator			Lights - Warning
	Alarms			Mast
	Battery Connector			Oil Leaks
	Belt			Oil Pressure
	Brakes - Parking			Overhead Guard
	Engine Oil Level			Radiator Level
	Forks			Safety Equipment
	Fuel			Steering
	Gauges			Tires
	Horn			Unusual Noises
	Hoses			Other: _____

Notes: _____
_____
_____
_____
_____
_____

Operator's Name

_____

Operator's Signature

_____

Supervisor's Name

_____

Supervisor's Signature

_____

PROPANE FORKLIFT INSPECTION CHECKLIST

Date: _____ Shift: _____

Forklift Serial Number: _____

Hour Meter Start: _____ End: _____ Total Hours: _____

	Gas gauge		Hour Meter
	LPG tank and locator pin		Hydraulic Controls
	LPG tank hose		Lights - Head and Tail
	Accelerator		Lights - Warning
	Alarms		Mast
	Battery Connector		Oil Leaks
	Belt		Oil Pressure
	Brakes - Parking		Overhead Guard
	Engine Oil Level		Radiator Level
	Forks		Safety Equipment
	Fuel		Steering
	Gauges		Tires
	Horn		Unusual Noises
	Hoses		Other: _____

Notes: _____
_____
_____
_____
_____
_____

Operator's Name	Supervisor's Name
_____	_____
Operator's Signature	Supervisor's Signature
_____	_____

PROPANE FORKLIFT INSPECTION CHECKLIST

Date: _____ Shift: _____

Forklift Serial Number: _____

Hour Meter Start: _____ End: _____ Total Hours: _____

	Gas gauge		Hour Meter
	LPG tank and locator pin		Hydraulic Controls
	LPG tank hose		Lights - Head and Tail
	Accelerator		Lights - Warning
	Alarms		Mast
	Battery Connector		Oil Leaks
	Belt		Oil Pressure
	Brakes - Parking		Overhead Guard
	Engine Oil Level		Radiator Level
	Forks		Safety Equipment
	Fuel		Steering
	Gauges		Tires
	Horn		Unusual Noises
	Hoses		Other: _____

Notes: _____
_____
_____
_____
_____
_____

Operator's Name

_____

Operator's Signature

_____

Supervisor's Name

_____

Supervisor's Signature

_____

PROPANE FORKLIFT INSPECTION CHECKLIST

Date: _____ Shift: _____

Forklift Serial Number: _____

Hour Meter Start: _____ End: _____ Total Hours: _____

	Gas gauge		Hour Meter
	LPG tank and locator pin		Hydraulic Controls
	LPG tank hose		Lights - Head and Tail
	Accelerator		Lights - Warning
	Alarms		Mast
	Battery Connector		Oil Leaks
	Belt		Oil Pressure
	Brakes - Parking		Overhead Guard
	Engine Oil Level		Radiator Level
	Forks		Safety Equipment
	Fuel		Steering
	Gauges		Tires
	Horn		Unusual Noises
	Hoses		Other: _____

Notes: _____
_____
_____
_____
_____
_____

Operator's Name

_____

Operator's Signature

_____

Supervisor's Name

_____

Supervisor's Signature

_____

PROPANE FORKLIFT INSPECTION CHECKLIST

Date: _____ Shift: _____

Forklift Serial Number: _____

Hour Meter Start: _____ End: _____ Total Hours: _____

	Gas gauge		Hour Meter
	LPG tank and locator pin		Hydraulic Controls
	LPG tank hose		Lights - Head and Tail
	Accelerator		Lights - Warning
	Alarms		Mast
	Battery Connector		Oil Leaks
	Belt		Oil Pressure
	Brakes - Parking		Overhead Guard
	Engine Oil Level		Radiator Level
	Forks		Safety Equipment
	Fuel		Steering
	Gauges		Tires
	Horn		Unusual Noises
	Hoses		Other: _____

Notes: _____
_____
_____
_____
_____
_____

Operator's Name	Supervisor's Name
_____	_____
Operator's Signature	Supervisor's Signature
_____	_____

PROPANE FORKLIFT INSPECTION CHECKLIST

Date: _____ Shift: _____

Forklift Serial Number: _____

Hour Meter Start: _____ End: _____ Total Hours: _____

Gas gauge		Hour Meter
LPG tank and locator pin		Hydraulic Controls
LPG tank hose		Lights - Head and Tail
Accelerator		Lights - Warning
Alarms		Mast
Battery Connector		Oil Leaks
Belt		Oil Pressure
Brakes - Parking		Overhead Guard
Engine Oil Level		Radiator Level
Forks		Safety Equipment
Fuel		Steering
Gauges		Tires
Horn		Unusual Noises
Hoses		Other: _____

Notes: _____
_____
_____
_____
_____
_____

Operator's Name	Supervisor's Name
_____	_____
Operator's Signature	Supervisor's Signature

PROPANE FORKLIFT INSPECTION CHECKLIST

Date: _____ Shift: _____

Forklift Serial Number: _____

Hour Meter Start: _____ End: _____ Total Hours: _____

	Gas gauge		Hour Meter
	LPG tank and locator pin		Hydraulic Controls
	LPG tank hose		Lights - Head and Tail
	Accelerator		Lights - Warning
	Alarms		Mast
	Battery Connector		Oil Leaks
	Belt		Oil Pressure
	Brakes - Parking		Overhead Guard
	Engine Oil Level		Radiator Level
	Forks		Safety Equipment
	Fuel		Steering
	Gauges		Tires
	Horn		Unusual Noises
	Hoses		Other: _____

Notes: _____
_____
_____
_____
_____
_____

Operator's Name	Supervisor's Name
_____	_____
Operator's Signature	Supervisor's Signature
_____	_____

PROPANE FORKLIFT INSPECTION CHECKLIST

Date: _____ Shift: _____

Forklift Serial Number: _____

Hour Meter Start: _____ End: _____ Total Hours: _____

	Gas gauge		Hour Meter
	LPG tank and locator pin		Hydraulic Controls
	LPG tank hose		Lights - Head and Tail
	Accelerator		Lights - Warning
	Alarms		Mast
	Battery Connector		Oil Leaks
	Belt		Oil Pressure
	Brakes - Parking		Overhead Guard
	Engine Oil Level		Radiator Level
	Forks		Safety Equipment
	Fuel		Steering
	Gauges		Tires
	Horn		Unusual Noises
	Hoses		Other: _____

Notes: _____

_____

_____

_____

_____

_____

Operator's Name	Supervisor's Name
_____	_____
Operator's Signature	Supervisor's Signature
_____	_____

PROPANE FORKLIFT INSPECTION CHECKLIST

Date: _____ Shift: _____

Forklift Serial Number: _____

Hour Meter Start: _____ End: _____ Total Hours: _____

	Gas gauge		Hour Meter
	LPG tank and locator pin		Hydraulic Controls
	LPG tank hose		Lights - Head and Tail
	Accelerator		Lights - Warning
	Alarms		Mast
	Battery Connector		Oil Leaks
	Belt		Oil Pressure
	Brakes - Parking		Overhead Guard
	Engine Oil Level		Radiator Level
	Forks		Safety Equipment
	Fuel		Steering
	Gauges		Tires
	Horn		Unusual Noises
	Hoses		Other: _____

Notes: _____
_____
_____
_____
_____
_____

Operator's Name

_____

Operator's Signature

_____

Supervisor's Name

_____

Supervisor's Signature

_____

PROPANE FORKLIFT INSPECTION CHECKLIST

Date: _____ Shift: _____

Forklift Serial Number: _____

Hour Meter Start: _____ End: _____ Total Hours: _____

	Gas gauge		Hour Meter
	LPG tank and locator pin		Hydraulic Controls
	LPG tank hose		Lights - Head and Tail
	Accelerator		Lights - Warning
	Alarms		Mast
	Battery Connector		Oil Leaks
	Belt		Oil Pressure
	Brakes - Parking		Overhead Guard
	Engine Oil Level		Radiator Level
	Forks		Safety Equipment
	Fuel		Steering
	Gauges		Tires
	Horn		Unusual Noises
	Hoses		Other: _____

Notes: _____

_____

_____

_____

_____

_____

Operator's Name

_____

Operator's Signature

_____

Supervisor's Name

_____

Supervisor's Signature

_____

PROPANE FORKLIFT INSPECTION CHECKLIST

Date: _____ Shift: _____

Forklift Serial Number: _____

Hour Meter Start: _____ End: _____ Total Hours: _____

	Gas gauge		Hour Meter
	LPG tank and locator pin		Hydraulic Controls
	LPG tank hose		Lights - Head and Tail
	Accelerator		Lights - Warning
	Alarms		Mast
	Battery Connector		Oil Leaks
	Belt		Oil Pressure
	Brakes - Parking		Overhead Guard
	Engine Oil Level		Radiator Level
	Forks		Safety Equipment
	Fuel		Steering
	Gauges		Tires
	Horn		Unusual Noises
	Hoses		Other: _____

Notes: _____
_____
_____
_____
_____
_____

Operator's Name

_____

Operator's Signature

_____

Supervisor's Name

_____

Supervisor's Signature

_____

PROPANE FORKLIFT INSPECTION CHECKLIST

Date: _____ Shift: _____

Forklift Serial Number: _____

Hour Meter Start: _____ End: _____ Total Hours: _____

	Gas gauge		Hour Meter
	LPG tank and locator pin		Hydraulic Controls
	LPG tank hose		Lights - Head and Tail
	Accelerator		Lights - Warning
	Alarms		Mast
	Battery Connector		Oil Leaks
	Belt		Oil Pressure
	Brakes - Parking		Overhead Guard
	Engine Oil Level		Radiator Level
	Forks		Safety Equipment
	Fuel		Steering
	Gauges		Tires
	Horn		Unusual Noises
	Hoses		Other: _____

Notes: _____
_____
_____
_____
_____
_____

Operator's Name

_____

Operator's Signature

_____

Supervisor's Name

_____

Supervisor's Signature

_____

PROPANE FORKLIFT INSPECTION CHECKLIST

Date: _____ Shift: _____

Forklift Serial Number: _____

Hour Meter Start: _____ End: _____ Total Hours: _____

	Gas gauge		Hour Meter
	LPG tank and locator pin		Hydraulic Controls
	LPG tank hose		Lights - Head and Tail
	Accelerator		Lights - Warning
	Alarms		Mast
	Battery Connector		Oil Leaks
	Belt		Oil Pressure
	Brakes - Parking		Overhead Guard
	Engine Oil Level		Radiator Level
	Forks		Safety Equipment
	Fuel		Steering
	Gauges		Tires
	Horn		Unusual Noises
	Hoses		Other: _____

Notes: _____
_____
_____
_____
_____
_____

Operator's Name

_____

Operator's Signature

_____

Supervisor's Name

_____

Supervisor's Signature

_____

PROPANE FORKLIFT INSPECTION CHECKLIST

Date: _____ Shift: _____

Forklift Serial Number: _____

Hour Meter Start: _____ End: _____ Total Hours: _____

	Gas gauge		Hour Meter
	LPG tank and locator pin		Hydraulic Controls
	LPG tank hose		Lights - Head and Tail
	Accelerator		Lights - Warning
	Alarms		Mast
	Battery Connector		Oil Leaks
	Belt		Oil Pressure
	Brakes - Parking		Overhead Guard
	Engine Oil Level		Radiator Level
	Forks		Safety Equipment
	Fuel		Steering
	Gauges		Tires
	Horn		Unusual Noises
	Hoses		Other: _____

Notes: _____
_____
_____
_____
_____
_____
_____

Operator's Name

_____

Operator's Signature

_____

Supervisor's Name

_____

Supervisor's Signature

_____

PROPANE FORKLIFT INSPECTION CHECKLIST

Date: _____ Shift: _____

Forklift Serial Number: _____

Hour Meter Start: _____ End: _____ Total Hours: _____

	Gas gauge		Hour Meter
	LPG tank and locator pin		Hydraulic Controls
	LPG tank hose		Lights - Head and Tail
	Accelerator		Lights - Warning
	Alarms		Mast
	Battery Connector		Oil Leaks
	Belt		Oil Pressure
	Brakes - Parking		Overhead Guard
	Engine Oil Level		Radiator Level
	Forks		Safety Equipment
	Fuel		Steering
	Gauges		Tires
	Horn		Unusual Noises
	Hoses		Other: _____

Notes: _____

_____

_____

_____

_____

_____

Operator's Name	Supervisor's Name
_____	_____
Operator's Signature	Supervisor's Signature
_____	_____

PROPANE FORKLIFT INSPECTION CHECKLIST

Date: _____ Shift: _____

Forklift Serial Number: _____

Hour Meter Start: _____ End: _____ Total Hours: _____

	Gas gauge		Hour Meter
	LPG tank and locator pin		Hydraulic Controls
	LPG tank hose		Lights - Head and Tail
	Accelerator		Lights - Warning
	Alarms		Mast
	Battery Connector		Oil Leaks
	Belt		Oil Pressure
	Brakes - Parking		Overhead Guard
	Engine Oil Level		Radiator Level
	Forks		Safety Equipment
	Fuel		Steering
	Gauges		Tires
	Horn		Unusual Noises
	Hoses		Other: _____

Notes: _____
_____
_____
_____
_____
_____

Operator's Name

_____

Operator's Signature

_____

Supervisor's Name

_____

Supervisor's Signature

_____

PROPANE FORKLIFT INSPECTION CHECKLIST

Date: _____ Shift: _____

Forklift Serial Number: _____

Hour Meter Start: _____ End: _____ Total Hours: _____

	Gas gauge		Hour Meter
	LPG tank and locator pin		Hydraulic Controls
	LPG tank hose		Lights - Head and Tail
	Accelerator		Lights - Warning
	Alarms		Mast
	Battery Connector		Oil Leaks
	Belt		Oil Pressure
	Brakes - Parking		Overhead Guard
	Engine Oil Level		Radiator Level
	Forks		Safety Equipment
	Fuel		Steering
	Gauges		Tires
	Horn		Unusual Noises
	Hoses		Other: _____

Notes: _____
_____
_____
_____
_____
_____
_____

Operator's Name

_____

Operator's Signature

_____

Supervisor's Name

_____

Supervisor's Signature

_____

PROPANE FORKLIFT INSPECTION CHECKLIST

Date: _____ Shift: _____

Forklift Serial Number: _____

Hour Meter Start: _____ End: _____ Total Hours: _____

	Gas gauge		Hour Meter
	LPG tank and locator pin		Hydraulic Controls
	LPG tank hose		Lights - Head and Tail
	Accelerator		Lights - Warning
	Alarms		Mast
	Battery Connector		Oil Leaks
	Belt		Oil Pressure
	Brakes - Parking		Overhead Guard
	Engine Oil Level		Radiator Level
	Forks		Safety Equipment
	Fuel		Steering
	Gauges		Tires
	Horn		Unusual Noises
	Hoses		Other: _____

Notes: _____
_____
_____
_____
_____
_____

Operator's Name	Supervisor's Name
_____	_____
Operator's Signature	Supervisor's Signature
_____	_____

PROPANE FORKLIFT INSPECTION CHECKLIST

Date: _____ Shift: _____

Forklift Serial Number: _____

Hour Meter Start: _____ End: _____ Total Hours: _____

	Gas gauge		Hour Meter
	LPG tank and locator pin		Hydraulic Controls
	LPG tank hose		Lights - Head and Tail
	Accelerator		Lights - Warning
	Alarms		Mast
	Battery Connector		Oil Leaks
	Belt		Oil Pressure
	Brakes - Parking		Overhead Guard
	Engine Oil Level		Radiator Level
	Forks		Safety Equipment
	Fuel		Steering
	Gauges		Tires
	Horn		Unusual Noises
	Hoses		Other: _____

Notes: _____
_____
_____
_____
_____
_____

Operator's Name	Supervisor's Name
_____	_____
Operator's Signature	Supervisor's Signature
_____	_____

PROPANE FORKLIFT INSPECTION CHECKLIST

Date: _____ Shift: _____

Forklift Serial Number: _____

Hour Meter Start:_____ End:_____ Total Hours:_____

	Gas gauge		Hour Meter
	LPG tank and locator pin		Hydraulic Controls
	LPG tank hose		Lights - Head and Tail
	Accelerator		Lights - Warning
	Alarms		Mast
	Battery Connector		Oil Leaks
	Belt		Oil Pressure
	Brakes - Parking		Overhead Guard
	Engine Oil Level		Radiator Level
	Forks		Safety Equipment
	Fuel		Steering
	Gauges		Tires
	Horn		Unusual Noises
	Hoses		Other: _____

Notes: _____
_____
_____
_____
_____
_____

Operator's Name

_____

Operator's Signature

_____

Supervisor's Name

_____

Supervisor's Signature

_____

PROPANE FORKLIFT INSPECTION CHECKLIST

Date: _____ Shift: _____

Forklift Serial Number: _____

Hour Meter Start: _____ End: _____ Total Hours: _____

	Gas gauge		Hour Meter
	LPG tank and locator pin		Hydraulic Controls
	LPG tank hose		Lights - Head and Tail
	Accelerator		Lights - Warning
	Alarms		Mast
	Battery Connector		Oil Leaks
	Belt		Oil Pressure
	Brakes - Parking		Overhead Guard
	Engine Oil Level		Radiator Level
	Forks		Safety Equipment
	Fuel		Steering
	Gauges		Tires
	Horn		Unusual Noises
	Hoses		Other: _____

Notes: _____
_____
_____
_____
_____
_____

Operator's Name	Supervisor's Name
_____	_____
Operator's Signature	Supervisor's Signature
_____	_____

PROPANE FORKLIFT INSPECTION CHECKLIST

Date: _____ Shift: _____

Forklift Serial Number: _____

Hour Meter Start: _____ End: _____ Total Hours: _____

	Gas gauge		Hour Meter
	LPG tank and locator pin		Hydraulic Controls
	LPG tank hose		Lights - Head and Tail
	Accelerator		Lights - Warning
	Alarms		Mast
	Battery Connector		Oil Leaks
	Belt		Oil Pressure
	Brakes - Parking		Overhead Guard
	Engine Oil Level		Radiator Level
	Forks		Safety Equipment
	Fuel		Steering
	Gauges		Tires
	Horn		Unusual Noises
	Hoses		Other: _____

Notes: _____

_____

_____

_____

_____

_____

Operator's Name

_____

Operator's Signature

_____

Supervisor's Name

_____

Supervisor's Signature

_____

PROPANE FORKLIFT INSPECTION CHECKLIST

Date: _____ Shift: _____

Forklift Serial Number: _____

Hour Meter Start: _____ End: _____ Total Hours: _____

	Gas gauge		Hour Meter
	LPG tank and locator pin		Hydraulic Controls
	LPG tank hose		Lights - Head and Tail
	Accelerator		Lights - Warning
	Alarms		Mast
	Battery Connector		Oil Leaks
	Belt		Oil Pressure
	Brakes - Parking		Overhead Guard
	Engine Oil Level		Radiator Level
	Forks		Safety Equipment
	Fuel		Steering
	Gauges		Tires
	Horn		Unusual Noises
	Hoses		Other: _____

Notes: _____
_____
_____
_____
_____
_____

Operator's Name	Supervisor's Name
_____	_____
Operator's Signature	Supervisor's Signature
_____	_____

PROPANE FORKLIFT INSPECTION CHECKLIST

Date: _____ Shift: _____

Forklift Serial Number: _____

Hour Meter Start: _____ End: _____ Total Hours: _____

	Gas gauge		Hour Meter
	LPG tank and locator pin		Hydraulic Controls
	LPG tank hose		Lights - Head and Tail
	Accelerator		Lights - Warning
	Alarms		Mast
	Battery Connector		Oil Leaks
	Belt		Oil Pressure
	Brakes - Parking		Overhead Guard
	Engine Oil Level		Radiator Level
	Forks		Safety Equipment
	Fuel		Steering
	Gauges		Tires
	Horn		Unusual Noises
	Hoses		Other: _____

Notes: _____
_____
_____
_____
_____
_____

Operator's Name

_____

Operator's Signature

_____

Supervisor's Name

_____

Supervisor's Signature

_____

PROPANE FORKLIFT INSPECTION CHECKLIST

Date: _____ Shift: _____

Forklift Serial Number: _____

Hour Meter Start: _____ End: _____ Total Hours: _____

	Gas gauge		Hour Meter
	LPG tank and locator pin		Hydraulic Controls
	LPG tank hose		Lights - Head and Tail
	Accelerator		Lights - Warning
	Alarms		Mast
	Battery Connector		Oil Leaks
	Belt		Oil Pressure
	Brakes - Parking		Overhead Guard
	Engine Oil Level		Radiator Level
	Forks		Safety Equipment
	Fuel		Steering
	Gauges		Tires
	Horn		Unusual Noises
	Hoses		Other: _____

Notes: _____
_____
_____
_____
_____
_____

Operator's Name	Supervisor's Name
Operator's Signature	Supervisor's Signature

PROPANE FORKLIFT INSPECTION CHECKLIST

Date: _____ Shift: _____

Forklift Serial Number: _____

Hour Meter Start: _____ End: _____ Total Hours: _____

	Gas gauge		Hour Meter
	LPG tank and locator pin		Hydraulic Controls
	LPG tank hose		Lights - Head and Tail
	Accelerator		Lights - Warning
	Alarms		Mast
	Battery Connector		Oil Leaks
	Belt		Oil Pressure
	Brakes - Parking		Overhead Guard
	Engine Oil Level		Radiator Level
	Forks		Safety Equipment
	Fuel		Steering
	Gauges		Tires
	Horn		Unusual Noises
	Hoses		Other: _____

Notes: _____
_____
_____
_____
_____
_____

Operator's Name

_____

Operator's Signature

_____

Supervisor's Name

_____

Supervisor's Signature

_____

PROPANE FORKLIFT INSPECTION CHECKLIST

Date: _____ Shift: _____

Forklift Serial Number: _____

Hour Meter Start: _____ End: _____ Total Hours: _____

	Gas gauge		Hour Meter
	LPG tank and locator pin		Hydraulic Controls
	LPG tank hose		Lights - Head and Tail
	Accelerator		Lights - Warning
	Alarms		Mast
	Battery Connector		Oil Leaks
	Belt		Oil Pressure
	Brakes - Parking		Overhead Guard
	Engine Oil Level		Radiator Level
	Forks		Safety Equipment
	Fuel		Steering
	Gauges		Tires
	Horn		Unusual Noises
	Hoses		Other: _____

Notes: _____
_____
_____
_____
_____
_____

Operator's Name	Supervisor's Name
_____	_____
Operator's Signature	Supervisor's Signature
_____	_____

PROPANE FORKLIFT INSPECTION CHECKLIST

Date: _____ Shift: _____

Forklift Serial Number: _____

Hour Meter Start:_____ End:_____ Total Hours:_____

Gas gauge		Hour Meter	
LPG tank and locator pin		Hydraulic Controls	
LPG tank hose		Lights - Head and Tail	
Accelerator		Lights - Warning	
Alarms		Mast	
Battery Connector		Oil Leaks	
Belt		Oil Pressure	
Brakes - Parking		Overhead Guard	
Engine Oil Level		Radiator Level	
Forks		Safety Equipment	
Fuel		Steering	
Gauges		Tires	
Horn		Unusual Noises	
Hoses		Other: _____	

Notes: _____
_____
_____
_____
_____
_____

Operator's Name	Supervisor's Name
_____	_____
Operator's Signature	Supervisor's Signature
_____	_____

PROPANE FORKLIFT INSPECTION CHECKLIST

Date: _____ Shift: _____

Forklift Serial Number: _____

Hour Meter Start: _____ End: _____ Total Hours: _____

	Gas gauge		Hour Meter
	LPG tank and locator pin		Hydraulic Controls
	LPG tank hose		Lights - Head and Tail
	Accelerator		Lights - Warning
	Alarms		Mast
	Battery Connector		Oil Leaks
	Belt		Oil Pressure
	Brakes - Parking		Overhead Guard
	Engine Oil Level		Radiator Level
	Forks		Safety Equipment
	Fuel		Steering
	Gauges		Tires
	Horn		Unusual Noises
	Hoses		Other: _____

Notes: _____
_____
_____
_____
_____
_____

Operator's Name	Supervisor's Name
_____	_____
Operator's Signature	Supervisor's Signature
_____	_____

PROPANE FORKLIFT INSPECTION CHECKLIST

Date: _____ Shift: _____

Forklift Serial Number: _____

Hour Meter Start: _____ End: _____ Total Hours: _____

	Gas gauge		Hour Meter
	LPG tank and locator pin		Hydraulic Controls
	LPG tank hose		Lights - Head and Tail
	Accelerator		Lights - Warning
	Alarms		Mast
	Battery Connector		Oil Leaks
	Belt		Oil Pressure
	Brakes - Parking		Overhead Guard
	Engine Oil Level		Radiator Level
	Forks		Safety Equipment
	Fuel		Steering
	Gauges		Tires
	Horn		Unusual Noises
	Hoses		Other: _____

Notes: _____
_____
_____
_____
_____
_____
_____

Operator's Name

_____

Operator's Signature

_____

Supervisor's Name

_____

Supervisor's Signature

_____

PROPANE FORKLIFT INSPECTION CHECKLIST

Date: _____ Shift: _____

Forklift Serial Number: _____

Hour Meter Start: _____ End: _____ Total Hours: _____

	Gas gauge			Hour Meter
	LPG tank and locator pin			Hydraulic Controls
	LPG tank hose			Lights - Head and Tail
	Accelerator			Lights - Warning
	Alarms			Mast
	Battery Connector			Oil Leaks
	Belt			Oil Pressure
	Brakes - Parking			Overhead Guard
	Engine Oil Level			Radiator Level
	Forks			Safety Equipment
	Fuel			Steering
	Gauges			Tires
	Horn			Unusual Noises
	Hoses			Other: _____

Notes: _____
_____
_____
_____
_____
_____

Operator's Name

_____

Operator's Signature

_____

Supervisor's Name

_____

Supervisor's Signature

_____

PROPANE FORKLIFT INSPECTION CHECKLIST

Date: _____ Shift: _____

Forklift Serial Number: _____

Hour Meter Start: _____ End: _____ Total Hours: _____

	Gas gauge		Hour Meter
	LPG tank and locator pin		Hydraulic Controls
	LPG tank hose		Lights - Head and Tail
	Accelerator		Lights - Warning
	Alarms		Mast
	Battery Connector		Oil Leaks
	Belt		Oil Pressure
	Brakes - Parking		Overhead Guard
	Engine Oil Level		Radiator Level
	Forks		Safety Equipment
	Fuel		Steering
	Gauges		Tires
	Horn		Unusual Noises
	Hoses		Other: _____

Notes: _____
_____
_____
_____
_____
_____

Operator's Name	Supervisor's Name
_____	_____
Operator's Signature	Supervisor's Signature
_____	_____

PROPANE FORKLIFT INSPECTION CHECKLIST

Date: _____ Shift: _____

Forklift Serial Number: _____

Hour Meter Start: _____ End: _____ Total Hours: _____

	Gas gauge		Hour Meter
	LPG tank and locator pin		Hydraulic Controls
	LPG tank hose		Lights - Head and Tail
	Accelerator		Lights - Warning
	Alarms		Mast
	Battery Connector		Oil Leaks
	Belt		Oil Pressure
	Brakes - Parking		Overhead Guard
	Engine Oil Level		Radiator Level
	Forks		Safety Equipment
	Fuel		Steering
	Gauges		Tires
	Horn		Unusual Noises
	Hoses		Other: _____

Notes: _____

_____

_____

_____

_____

_____

Operator's Name

_____

Operator's Signature

_____

Supervisor's Name

_____

Supervisor's Signature

_____

PROPANE FORKLIFT INSPECTION CHECKLIST

Date: _____ Shift: _____

Forklift Serial Number: _____

Hour Meter Start: _____ End: _____ Total Hours: _____

	Gas gauge		Hour Meter
	LPG tank and locator pin		Hydraulic Controls
	LPG tank hose		Lights - Head and Tail
	Accelerator		Lights - Warning
	Alarms		Mast
	Battery Connector		Oil Leaks
	Belt		Oil Pressure
	Brakes - Parking		Overhead Guard
	Engine Oil Level		Radiator Level
	Forks		Safety Equipment
	Fuel		Steering
	Gauges		Tires
	Horn		Unusual Noises
	Hoses		Other: _____

Notes: _____
_____
_____
_____
_____
_____

Operator's Name	Supervisor's Name
_____	_____
Operator's Signature	Supervisor's Signature
_____	_____

PROPANE FORKLIFT INSPECTION CHECKLIST

Date: _____ Shift: _____

Forklift Serial Number: _____

Hour Meter Start: _____ End: _____ Total Hours: _____

	Gas gauge		Hour Meter
	LPG tank and locator pin		Hydraulic Controls
	LPG tank hose		Lights - Head and Tail
	Accelerator		Lights - Warning
	Alarms		Mast
	Battery Connector		Oil Leaks
	Belt		Oil Pressure
	Brakes - Parking		Overhead Guard
	Engine Oil Level		Radiator Level
	Forks		Safety Equipment
	Fuel		Steering
	Gauges		Tires
	Horn		Unusual Noises
	Hoses		Other: _____

Notes: _____
_____
_____
_____
_____
_____

Operator's Name

_____

Operator's Signature

_____

Supervisor's Name

_____

Supervisor's Signature

_____

PROPANE FORKLIFT INSPECTION CHECKLIST

Date: _____ Shift: _____

Forklift Serial Number: _____

Hour Meter Start:_____ End:_____ Total Hours:_____

Gas gauge		Hour Meter
LPG tank and locator pin		Hydraulic Controls
LPG tank hose		Lights - Head and Tail
Accelerator		Lights - Warning
Alarms		Mast
Battery Connector		Oil Leaks
Belt		Oil Pressure
Brakes - Parking		Overhead Guard
Engine Oil Level		Radiator Level
Forks		Safety Equipment
Fuel		Steering
Gauges		Tires
Horn		Unusual Noises
Hoses		Other: _____

Notes: _____
_____
_____
_____
_____
_____

Operator's Name	Supervisor's Name
_____	_____
Operator's Signature	Supervisor's Signature
_____	_____

PROPANE FORKLIFT INSPECTION CHECKLIST

Date: _____ Shift: _____

Forklift Serial Number: _____

Hour Meter Start: _____ End: _____ Total Hours: _____

	Gas gauge		Hour Meter
	LPG tank and locator pin		Hydraulic Controls
	LPG tank hose		Lights - Head and Tail
	Accelerator		Lights - Warning
	Alarms		Mast
	Battery Connector		Oil Leaks
	Belt		Oil Pressure
	Brakes - Parking		Overhead Guard
	Engine Oil Level		Radiator Level
	Forks		Safety Equipment
	Fuel		Steering
	Gauges		Tires
	Horn		Unusual Noises
	Hoses		Other: _____

Notes: _____
_____
_____
_____
_____
_____
_____

Operator's Name

_____

Operator's Signature

_____

Supervisor's Name

_____

Supervisor's Signature

_____

PROPANE FORKLIFT INSPECTION CHECKLIST

Date: _____ Shift: _____

Forklift Serial Number: _____

Hour Meter Start: _____ End: _____ Total Hours: _____

	Gas gauge		Hour Meter
	LPG tank and locator pin		Hydraulic Controls
	LPG tank hose		Lights - Head and Tail
	Accelerator		Lights - Warning
	Alarms		Mast
	Battery Connector		Oil Leaks
	Belt		Oil Pressure
	Brakes - Parking		Overhead Guard
	Engine Oil Level		Radiator Level
	Forks		Safety Equipment
	Fuel		Steering
	Gauges		Tires
	Horn		Unusual Noises
	Hoses		Other: _____

Notes: _____
_____
_____
_____
_____
_____

Operator's Name	Supervisor's Name
_____	_____
Operator's Signature	Supervisor's Signature
_____	_____

PROPANE FORKLIFT INSPECTION CHECKLIST

Date: _____ Shift: _____

Forklift Serial Number: _____

Hour Meter Start: _____ End: _____ Total Hours: _____

	Gas gauge		Hour Meter
	LPG tank and locator pin		Hydraulic Controls
	LPG tank hose		Lights - Head and Tail
	Accelerator		Lights - Warning
	Alarms		Mast
	Battery Connector		Oil Leaks
	Belt		Oil Pressure
	Brakes - Parking		Overhead Guard
	Engine Oil Level		Radiator Level
	Forks		Safety Equipment
	Fuel		Steering
	Gauges		Tires
	Horn		Unusual Noises
	Hoses		Other: _____

Notes: _____
_____
_____
_____
_____
_____

Operator's Name

_____

Operator's Signature

_____

Supervisor's Name

_____

Supervisor's Signature

_____

PROPANE FORKLIFT INSPECTION CHECKLIST

Date: _____ Shift: _____

Forklift Serial Number: _____

Hour Meter Start: _____ End: _____ Total Hours: _____

	Gas gauge		Hour Meter
	LPG tank and locator pin		Hydraulic Controls
	LPG tank hose		Lights - Head and Tail
	Accelerator		Lights - Warning
	Alarms		Mast
	Battery Connector		Oil Leaks
	Belt		Oil Pressure
	Brakes - Parking		Overhead Guard
	Engine Oil Level		Radiator Level
	Forks		Safety Equipment
	Fuel		Steering
	Gauges		Tires
	Horn		Unusual Noises
	Hoses		Other: _____

Notes: _____
_____
_____
_____
_____
_____
_____

Operator's Name	Supervisor's Name
_____	_____
Operator's Signature	Supervisor's Signature
_____	_____

PROPANE FORKLIFT INSPECTION CHECKLIST

Date: _____ Shift: _____

Forklift Serial Number: _____

Hour Meter Start: _____ End: _____ Total Hours: _____

	Gas gauge		Hour Meter
	LPG tank and locator pin		Hydraulic Controls
	LPG tank hose		Lights - Head and Tail
	Accelerator		Lights - Warning
	Alarms		Mast
	Battery Connector		Oil Leaks
	Belt		Oil Pressure
	Brakes - Parking		Overhead Guard
	Engine Oil Level		Radiator Level
	Forks		Safety Equipment
	Fuel		Steering
	Gauges		Tires
	Horn		Unusual Noises
	Hoses		Other: _____

Notes: _____
_____
_____
_____
_____
_____

Operator's Name
_____
Operator's Signature
_____

Supervisor's Name
_____
Supervisor's Signature
_____

PROPANE FORKLIFT INSPECTION CHECKLIST

Date: _____ Shift: _____

Forklift Serial Number: _____

Hour Meter Start: _____ End: _____ Total Hours: _____

	Gas gauge		Hour Meter
	LPG tank and locator pin		Hydraulic Controls
	LPG tank hose		Lights - Head and Tail
	Accelerator		Lights - Warning
	Alarms		Mast
	Battery Connector		Oil Leaks
	Belt		Oil Pressure
	Brakes - Parking		Overhead Guard
	Engine Oil Level		Radiator Level
	Forks		Safety Equipment
	Fuel		Steering
	Gauges		Tires
	Horn		Unusual Noises
	Hoses		Other: _____

Notes: _____
_____
_____
_____
_____
_____

Operator's Name

_____

Operator's Signature

_____

Supervisor's Name

_____

Supervisor's Signature

_____

PROPANE FORKLIFT INSPECTION CHECKLIST

Date: _____ Shift: _____

Forklift Serial Number: _____

Hour Meter Start: _____ End: _____ Total Hours: _____

	Gas gauge		Hour Meter
	LPG tank and locator pin		Hydraulic Controls
	LPG tank hose		Lights - Head and Tail
	Accelerator		Lights - Warning
	Alarms		Mast
	Battery Connector		Oil Leaks
	Belt		Oil Pressure
	Brakes - Parking		Overhead Guard
	Engine Oil Level		Radiator Level
	Forks		Safety Equipment
	Fuel		Steering
	Gauges		Tires
	Horn		Unusual Noises
	Hoses		Other: _____

Notes: _____
_____
_____
_____
_____
_____

Operator's Name

_____

Operator's Signature

_____

Supervisor's Name

_____

Supervisor's Signature

_____

PROPANE FORKLIFT INSPECTION CHECKLIST

Date: _____ Shift: _____

Forklift Serial Number: _____

Hour Meter Start: _____ End: _____ Total Hours: _____

	Gas gauge		Hour Meter
	LPG tank and locator pin		Hydraulic Controls
	LPG tank hose		Lights - Head and Tail
	Accelerator		Lights - Warning
	Alarms		Mast
	Battery Connector		Oil Leaks
	Belt		Oil Pressure
	Brakes - Parking		Overhead Guard
	Engine Oil Level		Radiator Level
	Forks		Safety Equipment
	Fuel		Steering
	Gauges		Tires
	Horn		Unusual Noises
	Hoses		Other: _____

Notes: _____
_____
_____
_____
_____
_____

Operator's Name

_____

Operator's Signature

_____

Supervisor's Name

_____

Supervisor's Signature

_____

PROPANE FORKLIFT INSPECTION CHECKLIST

Date: _____ Shift: _____

Forklift Serial Number: _____

Hour Meter Start: _____ End: _____ Total Hours: _____

	Gas gauge		Hour Meter
	LPG tank and locator pin		Hydraulic Controls
	LPG tank hose		Lights - Head and Tail
	Accelerator		Lights - Warning
	Alarms		Mast
	Battery Connector		Oil Leaks
	Belt		Oil Pressure
	Brakes - Parking		Overhead Guard
	Engine Oil Level		Radiator Level
	Forks		Safety Equipment
	Fuel		Steering
	Gauges		Tires
	Horn		Unusual Noises
	Hoses		Other: _____

Notes: _____
_____
_____
_____
_____
_____

Operator's Name

_____

Operator's Signature

_____

Supervisor's Name

_____

Supervisor's Signature

_____

PROPANE FORKLIFT INSPECTION CHECKLIST

Date: _____ Shift: _____

Forklift Serial Number: _____

Hour Meter Start: _____ End: _____ Total Hours: _____

	Gas gauge		Hour Meter
	LPG tank and locator pin		Hydraulic Controls
	LPG tank hose		Lights - Head and Tail
	Accelerator		Lights - Warning
	Alarms		Mast
	Battery Connector		Oil Leaks
	Belt		Oil Pressure
	Brakes - Parking		Overhead Guard
	Engine Oil Level		Radiator Level
	Forks		Safety Equipment
	Fuel		Steering
	Gauges		Tires
	Horn		Unusual Noises
	Hoses		Other: _____

Notes: _____
_____
_____
_____
_____
_____
_____

Operator's Name

_____

Operator's Signature

_____

Supervisor's Name

_____

Supervisor's Signature

_____

PROPANE FORKLIFT INSPECTION CHECKLIST

Date: _____ Shift: _____

Forklift Serial Number: _____

Hour Meter Start:_____ End:_____ Total Hours:_____

	Gas gauge		Hour Meter
	LPG tank and locator pin		Hydraulic Controls
	LPG tank hose		Lights - Head and Tail
	Accelerator		Lights - Warning
	Alarms		Mast
	Battery Connector		Oil Leaks
	Belt		Oil Pressure
	Brakes - Parking		Overhead Guard
	Engine Oil Level		Radiator Level
	Forks		Safety Equipment
	Fuel		Steering
	Gauges		Tires
	Horn		Unusual Noises
	Hoses		Other: _____

Notes: _____
_____
_____
_____
_____
_____

Operator's Name	Supervisor's Name
_____	_____
Operator's Signature	Supervisor's Signature
_____	_____

PROPANE FORKLIFT INSPECTION CHECKLIST

Date: _____ Shift: _____

Forklift Serial Number: _____

Hour Meter Start: _____ End: _____ Total Hours: _____

	Gas gauge		Hour Meter
	LPG tank and locator pin		Hydraulic Controls
	LPG tank hose		Lights - Head and Tail
	Accelerator		Lights - Warning
	Alarms		Mast
	Battery Connector		Oil Leaks
	Belt		Oil Pressure
	Brakes - Parking		Overhead Guard
	Engine Oil Level		Radiator Level
	Forks		Safety Equipment
	Fuel		Steering
	Gauges		Tires
	Horn		Unusual Noises
	Hoses		Other: _____

Notes: _____
_____
_____
_____
_____
_____

Operator's Name

_____

Operator's Signature

_____

Supervisor's Name

_____

Supervisor's Signature

_____

PROPANE FORKLIFT INSPECTION CHECKLIST

Date: _____ Shift: _____

Forklift Serial Number: _____

Hour Meter Start: _____ End: _____ Total Hours: _____

	Gas gauge		Hour Meter
	LPG tank and locator pin		Hydraulic Controls
	LPG tank hose		Lights - Head and Tail
	Accelerator		Lights - Warning
	Alarms		Mast
	Battery Connector		Oil Leaks
	Belt		Oil Pressure
	Brakes - Parking		Overhead Guard
	Engine Oil Level		Radiator Level
	Forks		Safety Equipment
	Fuel		Steering
	Gauges		Tires
	Horn		Unusual Noises
	Hoses		Other: _____

Notes: _____
_____
_____
_____
_____
_____

Operator's Name	Supervisor's Name
Operator's Signature	Supervisor's Signature

PROPANE FORKLIFT INSPECTION CHECKLIST

Date: _____ Shift: _____

Forklift Serial Number: _____

Hour Meter Start: _____ End: _____ Total Hours: _____

	Gas gauge		Hour Meter
	LPG tank and locator pin		Hydraulic Controls
	LPG tank hose		Lights - Head and Tail
	Accelerator		Lights - Warning
	Alarms		Mast
	Battery Connector		Oil Leaks
	Belt		Oil Pressure
	Brakes - Parking		Overhead Guard
	Engine Oil Level		Radiator Level
	Forks		Safety Equipment
	Fuel		Steering
	Gauges		Tires
	Horn		Unusual Noises
	Hoses		Other: _____

Notes: _____
_____
_____
_____
_____
_____

Operator's Name	Supervisor's Name
_____	_____
Operator's Signature	Supervisor's Signature
_____	_____

PROPANE FORKLIFT INSPECTION CHECKLIST

Date: _____ Shift: _____

Forklift Serial Number: _____

Hour Meter Start: _____ End: _____ Total Hours: _____

	Gas gauge		Hour Meter
	LPG tank and locator pin		Hydraulic Controls
	LPG tank hose		Lights - Head and Tail
	Accelerator		Lights - Warning
	Alarms		Mast
	Battery Connector		Oil Leaks
	Belt		Oil Pressure
	Brakes - Parking		Overhead Guard
	Engine Oil Level		Radiator Level
	Forks		Safety Equipment
	Fuel		Steering
	Gauges		Tires
	Horn		Unusual Noises
	Hoses		Other: _____

Notes: _____
_____
_____
_____
_____
_____

Operator's Name
_____

Operator's Signature
_____

Supervisor's Name
_____

Supervisor's Signature
_____

PROPANE FORKLIFT INSPECTION CHECKLIST

Date: _____ Shift: _____

Forklift Serial Number: _____

Hour Meter Start: _____ End: _____ Total Hours: _____

	Gas gauge		Hour Meter
	LPG tank and locator pin		Hydraulic Controls
	LPG tank hose		Lights - Head and Tail
	Accelerator		Lights - Warning
	Alarms		Mast
	Battery Connector		Oil Leaks
	Belt		Oil Pressure
	Brakes - Parking		Overhead Guard
	Engine Oil Level		Radiator Level
	Forks		Safety Equipment
	Fuel		Steering
	Gauges		Tires
	Horn		Unusual Noises
	Hoses		Other: _____

Notes: _____
_____
_____
_____
_____
_____

Operator's Name

_____

Operator's Signature

_____

Supervisor's Name

_____

Supervisor's Signature

_____

PROPANE FORKLIFT INSPECTION CHECKLIST

Date: _____ Shift: _____

Forklift Serial Number: _____

Hour Meter Start:_____ End:_____ Total Hours:_____

	Gas gauge		Hour Meter
	LPG tank and locator pin		Hydraulic Controls
	LPG tank hose		Lights - Head and Tail
	Accelerator		Lights - Warning
	Alarms		Mast
	Battery Connector		Oil Leaks
	Belt		Oil Pressure
	Brakes - Parking		Overhead Guard
	Engine Oil Level		Radiator Level
	Forks		Safety Equipment
	Fuel		Steering
	Gauges		Tires
	Horn		Unusual Noises
	Hoses		Other: _____

Notes: _____
_____
_____
_____
_____
_____

Operator's Name

_____

Operator's Signature

_____

Supervisor's Name

_____

Supervisor's Signature

_____

PROPANE FORKLIFT INSPECTION CHECKLIST

Date: _____ Shift: _____

Forklift Serial Number: _____

Hour Meter Start: _____ End: _____ Total Hours: _____

	Gas gauge		Hour Meter
	LPG tank and locator pin		Hydraulic Controls
	LPG tank hose		Lights - Head and Tail
	Accelerator		Lights - Warning
	Alarms		Mast
	Battery Connector		Oil Leaks
	Belt		Oil Pressure
	Brakes - Parking		Overhead Guard
	Engine Oil Level		Radiator Level
	Forks		Safety Equipment
	Fuel		Steering
	Gauges		Tires
	Horn		Unusual Noises
	Hoses		Other: _____

Notes: _____
_____
_____
_____
_____
_____

Operator's Name	Supervisor's Name
_____	_____
Operator's Signature	Supervisor's Signature
_____	_____

PROPANE FORKLIFT INSPECTION CHECKLIST

Date: _____ Shift: _____

Forklift Serial Number: _____

Hour Meter Start: _____ End: _____ Total Hours: _____

	Gas gauge		Hour Meter
	LPG tank and locator pin		Hydraulic Controls
	LPG tank hose		Lights - Head and Tail
	Accelerator		Lights - Warning
	Alarms		Mast
	Battery Connector		Oil Leaks
	Belt		Oil Pressure
	Brakes - Parking		Overhead Guard
	Engine Oil Level		Radiator Level
	Forks		Safety Equipment
	Fuel		Steering
	Gauges		Tires
	Horn		Unusual Noises
	Hoses		Other: _____

Notes: _____
_____
_____
_____
_____
_____

Operator's Name

_____

Operator's Signature

_____

Supervisor's Name

_____

Supervisor's Signature

_____

PROPANE FORKLIFT INSPECTION CHECKLIST

Date: _____ Shift: _____

Forklift Serial Number: _____

Hour Meter Start: _____ End: _____ Total Hours: _____

	Gas gauge		Hour Meter
	LPG tank and locator pin		Hydraulic Controls
	LPG tank hose		Lights - Head and Tail
	Accelerator		Lights - Warning
	Alarms		Mast
	Battery Connector		Oil Leaks
	Belt		Oil Pressure
	Brakes - Parking		Overhead Guard
	Engine Oil Level		Radiator Level
	Forks		Safety Equipment
	Fuel		Steering
	Gauges		Tires
	Horn		Unusual Noises
	Hoses		Other: _____

Notes: _____
_____
_____
_____
_____
_____

Operator's Name	Supervisor's Name
Operator's Signature	Supervisor's Signature

PROPANE FORKLIFT INSPECTION CHECKLIST

Date: _____ Shift: _____

Forklift Serial Number: _____

Hour Meter Start:_____ End:_____ Total Hours:_____

	Gas gauge		Hour Meter
	LPG tank and locator pin		Hydraulic Controls
	LPG tank hose		Lights - Head and Tail
	Accelerator		Lights - Warning
	Alarms		Mast
	Battery Connector		Oil Leaks
	Belt		Oil Pressure
	Brakes - Parking		Overhead Guard
	Engine Oil Level		Radiator Level
	Forks		Safety Equipment
	Fuel		Steering
	Gauges		Tires
	Horn		Unusual Noises
	Hoses		Other: _____

Notes: _____
_____
_____
_____
_____
_____

Operator's Name

_____

Operator's Signature

_____

Supervisor's Name

_____

Supervisor's Signature

_____

PROPANE FORKLIFT INSPECTION CHECKLIST

Date: _____ Shift: _____

Forklift Serial Number: _____

Hour Meter Start: _____ End: _____ Total Hours: _____

	Gas gauge		Hour Meter
	LPG tank and locator pin		Hydraulic Controls
	LPG tank hose		Lights - Head and Tail
	Accelerator		Lights - Warning
	Alarms		Mast
	Battery Connector		Oil Leaks
	Belt		Oil Pressure
	Brakes - Parking		Overhead Guard
	Engine Oil Level		Radiator Level
	Forks		Safety Equipment
	Fuel		Steering
	Gauges		Tires
	Horn		Unusual Noises
	Hoses		Other: _____

Notes: _____
_____
_____
_____
_____
_____

Operator's Name	Supervisor's Name
_____	_____
Operator's Signature	Supervisor's Signature
_____	_____

PROPANE FORKLIFT INSPECTION CHECKLIST

Date: _____ Shift: _____

Forklift Serial Number: _____

Hour Meter Start: _____ End: _____ Total Hours: _____

	Gas gauge		Hour Meter
	LPG tank and locator pin		Hydraulic Controls
	LPG tank hose		Lights - Head and Tail
	Accelerator		Lights - Warning
	Alarms		Mast
	Battery Connector		Oil Leaks
	Belt		Oil Pressure
	Brakes - Parking		Overhead Guard
	Engine Oil Level		Radiator Level
	Forks		Safety Equipment
	Fuel		Steering
	Gauges		Tires
	Horn		Unusual Noises
	Hoses		Other: _____

Notes: _____
_____
_____
_____
_____
_____

Operator's Name	Supervisor's Name
_____	_____
Operator's Signature	Supervisor's Signature
_____	_____

PROPANE FORKLIFT INSPECTION CHECKLIST

Date: _____ Shift: _____

Forklift Serial Number: _____

Hour Meter Start: _____ End: _____ Total Hours: _____

	Gas gauge		Hour Meter
	LPG tank and locator pin		Hydraulic Controls
	LPG tank hose		Lights - Head and Tail
	Accelerator		Lights - Warning
	Alarms		Mast
	Battery Connector		Oil Leaks
	Belt		Oil Pressure
	Brakes - Parking		Overhead Guard
	Engine Oil Level		Radiator Level
	Forks		Safety Equipment
	Fuel		Steering
	Gauges		Tires
	Horn		Unusual Noises
	Hoses		Other: _____

Notes: _____
_____
_____
_____
_____
_____

Operator's Name	Supervisor's Name
_____	_____
Operator's Signature	Supervisor's Signature
_____	_____

PROPANE FORKLIFT INSPECTION CHECKLIST

Date: _____ Shift: _____

Forklift Serial Number: _____

Hour Meter Start: _____ End: _____ Total Hours: _____

	Gas gauge		Hour Meter
	LPG tank and locator pin		Hydraulic Controls
	LPG tank hose		Lights - Head and Tail
	Accelerator		Lights - Warning
	Alarms		Mast
	Battery Connector		Oil Leaks
	Belt		Oil Pressure
	Brakes - Parking		Overhead Guard
	Engine Oil Level		Radiator Level
	Forks		Safety Equipment
	Fuel		Steering
	Gauges		Tires
	Horn		Unusual Noises
	Hoses		Other: _____

Notes: _____
_____
_____
_____
_____
_____

Operator's Name	Supervisor's Name
Operator's Signature	Supervisor's Signature

PROPANE FORKLIFT INSPECTION CHECKLIST

Date: _____ Shift: _____

Forklift Serial Number: _____

Hour Meter Start: _____ End: _____ Total Hours: _____

	Gas gauge		Hour Meter
	LPG tank and locator pin		Hydraulic Controls
	LPG tank hose		Lights - Head and Tail
	Accelerator		Lights - Warning
	Alarms		Mast
	Battery Connector		Oil Leaks
	Belt		Oil Pressure
	Brakes - Parking		Overhead Guard
	Engine Oil Level		Radiator Level
	Forks		Safety Equipment
	Fuel		Steering
	Gauges		Tires
	Horn		Unusual Noises
	Hoses		Other: _____

Notes: _____

_____

_____

_____

_____

_____

Operator's Name	Supervisor's Name
Operator's Signature	Supervisor's Signature

PROPANE FORKLIFT INSPECTION CHECKLIST

Date: _____ Shift: _____

Forklift Serial Number: _____

Hour Meter Start: _____ End: _____ Total Hours: _____

	Gas gauge		Hour Meter
	LPG tank and locator pin		Hydraulic Controls
	LPG tank hose		Lights - Head and Tail
	Accelerator		Lights - Warning
	Alarms		Mast
	Battery Connector		Oil Leaks
	Belt		Oil Pressure
	Brakes - Parking		Overhead Guard
	Engine Oil Level		Radiator Level
	Forks		Safety Equipment
	Fuel		Steering
	Gauges		Tires
	Horn		Unusual Noises
	Hoses		Other: _____

Notes: _____
_____
_____
_____
_____
_____

Operator's Name

_____

Operator's Signature

_____

Supervisor's Name

_____

Supervisor's Signature

_____

PROPANE FORKLIFT INSPECTION CHECKLIST

Date: _____ Shift: _____

Forklift Serial Number: _____

Hour Meter Start:_____ End:_____ Total Hours:_____

Gas gauge		Hour Meter
LPG tank and locator pin		Hydraulic Controls
LPG tank hose		Lights - Head and Tail
Accelerator		Lights - Warning
Alarms		Mast
Battery Connector		Oil Leaks
Belt		Oil Pressure
Brakes - Parking		Overhead Guard
Engine Oil Level		Radiator Level
Forks		Safety Equipment
Fuel		Steering
Gauges		Tires
Horn		Unusual Noises
Hoses		Other: _____

Notes: _____
_____
_____
_____
_____
_____

Operator's Name	Supervisor's Name
Operator's Signature	Supervisor's Signature

PROPANE FORKLIFT INSPECTION CHECKLIST

Date: _____ Shift: _____

Forklift Serial Number: _____

Hour Meter Start: _____ End: _____ Total Hours: _____

	Gas gauge		Hour Meter
	LPG tank and locator pin		Hydraulic Controls
	LPG tank hose		Lights - Head and Tail
	Accelerator		Lights - Warning
	Alarms		Mast
	Battery Connector		Oil Leaks
	Belt		Oil Pressure
	Brakes - Parking		Overhead Guard
	Engine Oil Level		Radiator Level
	Forks		Safety Equipment
	Fuel		Steering
	Gauges		Tires
	Horn		Unusual Noises
	Hoses		Other: _____

Notes: _____
_____
_____
_____
_____
_____

Operator's Name	Supervisor's Name
_____	_____
Operator's Signature	Supervisor's Signature
_____	_____

PROPANE FORKLIFT INSPECTION CHECKLIST

Date: _____ Shift: _____

Forklift Serial Number: _____

Hour Meter Start: _____ End: _____ Total Hours: _____

Gas gauge		Hour Meter
LPG tank and locator pin		Hydraulic Controls
LPG tank hose		Lights - Head and Tail
Accelerator		Lights - Warning
Alarms		Mast
Battery Connector		Oil Leaks
Belt		Oil Pressure
Brakes - Parking		Overhead Guard
Engine Oil Level		Radiator Level
Forks		Safety Equipment
Fuel		Steering
Gauges		Tires
Horn		Unusual Noises
Hoses		Other: _____

Notes: _____
_____
_____
_____
_____
_____

Operator's Name	Supervisor's Name
Operator's Signature	Supervisor's Signature

PROPANE FORKLIFT INSPECTION CHECKLIST

Date: _____ Shift: _____

Forklift Serial Number: _____

Hour Meter Start: _____ End: _____ Total Hours: _____

	Gas gauge		Hour Meter
	LPG tank and locator pin		Hydraulic Controls
	LPG tank hose		Lights - Head and Tail
	Accelerator		Lights - Warning
	Alarms		Mast
	Battery Connector		Oil Leaks
	Belt		Oil Pressure
	Brakes - Parking		Overhead Guard
	Engine Oil Level		Radiator Level
	Forks		Safety Equipment
	Fuel		Steering
	Gauges		Tires
	Horn		Unusual Noises
	Hoses		Other: _____

Notes: _____
_____
_____
_____
_____
_____

Operator's Name	Supervisor's Name
Operator's Signature	Supervisor's Signature

PROPANE FORKLIFT INSPECTION CHECKLIST

Date: _____ Shift: _____

Forklift Serial Number: _____

Hour Meter Start: _____ End: _____ Total Hours: _____

	Gas gauge		Hour Meter
	LPG tank and locator pin		Hydraulic Controls
	LPG tank hose		Lights - Head and Tail
	Accelerator		Lights - Warning
	Alarms		Mast
	Battery Connector		Oil Leaks
	Belt		Oil Pressure
	Brakes - Parking		Overhead Guard
	Engine Oil Level		Radiator Level
	Forks		Safety Equipment
	Fuel		Steering
	Gauges		Tires
	Horn		Unusual Noises
	Hoses		Other: _____

Notes: _____
_____
_____
_____
_____
_____

Operator's Name

_____

Operator's Signature

_____

Supervisor's Name

_____

Supervisor's Signature

_____

PROPANE FORKLIFT INSPECTION CHECKLIST

Date: _____ Shift: _____

Forklift Serial Number: _____

Hour Meter Start: _____ End: _____ Total Hours: _____

	Gas gauge		Hour Meter
	LPG tank and locator pin		Hydraulic Controls
	LPG tank hose		Lights - Head and Tail
	Accelerator		Lights - Warning
	Alarms		Mast
	Battery Connector		Oil Leaks
	Belt		Oil Pressure
	Brakes - Parking		Overhead Guard
	Engine Oil Level		Radiator Level
	Forks		Safety Equipment
	Fuel		Steering
	Gauges		Tires
	Horn		Unusual Noises
	Hoses		Other: _____

Notes: _____
_____
_____
_____
_____
_____

Operator's Name	Supervisor's Name
_____	_____
Operator's Signature	Supervisor's Signature
_____	_____

PROPANE FORKLIFT INSPECTION CHECKLIST

Date: _____ Shift: _____

Forklift Serial Number: _____

Hour Meter Start: _____ End: _____ Total Hours: _____

	Gas gauge		Hour Meter
	LPG tank and locator pin		Hydraulic Controls
	LPG tank hose		Lights - Head and Tail
	Accelerator		Lights - Warning
	Alarms		Mast
	Battery Connector		Oil Leaks
	Belt		Oil Pressure
	Brakes - Parking		Overhead Guard
	Engine Oil Level		Radiator Level
	Forks		Safety Equipment
	Fuel		Steering
	Gauges		Tires
	Horn		Unusual Noises
	Hoses		Other: _____

Notes: _____
_____
_____
_____
_____
_____

Operator's Name

_____

Operator's Signature

_____

Supervisor's Name

_____

Supervisor's Signature

_____

PROPANE FORKLIFT INSPECTION CHECKLIST

Date: _____ Shift: _____

Forklift Serial Number: _____

Hour Meter Start: _____ End: _____ Total Hours: _____

	Gas gauge		Hour Meter
	LPG tank and locator pin		Hydraulic Controls
	LPG tank hose		Lights - Head and Tail
	Accelerator		Lights - Warning
	Alarms		Mast
	Battery Connector		Oil Leaks
	Belt		Oil Pressure
	Brakes - Parking		Overhead Guard
	Engine Oil Level		Radiator Level
	Forks		Safety Equipment
	Fuel		Steering
	Gauges		Tires
	Horn		Unusual Noises
	Hoses		Other: _____

Notes: _____
_____
_____
_____
_____
_____
_____

Operator's Name

_____

Operator's Signature

_____

Supervisor's Name

_____

Supervisor's Signature

_____

PROPANE FORKLIFT INSPECTION CHECKLIST

Date: _____ Shift: _____

Forklift Serial Number: _____

Hour Meter Start: _____ End: _____ Total Hours: _____

Gas gauge		Hour Meter
LPG tank and locator pin		Hydraulic Controls
LPG tank hose		Lights - Head and Tail
Accelerator		Lights - Warning
Alarms		Mast
Battery Connector		Oil Leaks
Belt		Oil Pressure
Brakes - Parking		Overhead Guard
Engine Oil Level		Radiator Level
Forks		Safety Equipment
Fuel		Steering
Gauges		Tires
Horn		Unusual Noises
Hoses		Other: _____

Notes: _____
_____
_____
_____
_____
_____

Operator's Name	Supervisor's Name
_____	_____
Operator's Signature	Supervisor's Signature
_____	_____

PROPANE FORKLIFT INSPECTION CHECKLIST

Date: _____ Shift: _____

Forklift Serial Number: _____

Hour Meter Start: _____ End: _____ Total Hours: _____

	Gas gauge		Hour Meter
	LPG tank and locator pin		Hydraulic Controls
	LPG tank hose		Lights - Head and Tail
	Accelerator		Lights - Warning
	Alarms		Mast
	Battery Connector		Oil Leaks
	Belt		Oil Pressure
	Brakes - Parking		Overhead Guard
	Engine Oil Level		Radiator Level
	Forks		Safety Equipment
	Fuel		Steering
	Gauges		Tires
	Horn		Unusual Noises
	Hoses		Other: _____

Notes: _____
_____
_____
_____
_____
_____
_____

Operator's Name	Supervisor's Name
_____	_____
Operator's Signature	Supervisor's Signature
_____	_____

PROPANE FORKLIFT INSPECTION CHECKLIST

Date: _____ Shift: _____

Forklift Serial Number: _____

Hour Meter Start: _____ End: _____ Total Hours: _____

	Gas gauge		Hour Meter
	LPG tank and locator pin		Hydraulic Controls
	LPG tank hose		Lights - Head and Tail
	Accelerator		Lights - Warning
	Alarms		Mast
	Battery Connector		Oil Leaks
	Belt		Oil Pressure
	Brakes - Parking		Overhead Guard
	Engine Oil Level		Radiator Level
	Forks		Safety Equipment
	Fuel		Steering
	Gauges		Tires
	Horn		Unusual Noises
	Hoses		Other: _____

Notes: _____
_____
_____
_____
_____
_____

Operator's Name

_____

Operator's Signature

_____

Supervisor's Name

_____

Supervisor's Signature

_____

PROPANE FORKLIFT INSPECTION CHECKLIST

Date: _____ Shift: _____

Forklift Serial Number: _____

Hour Meter Start: _____ End: _____ Total Hours: _____

	Gas gauge		Hour Meter
	LPG tank and locator pin		Hydraulic Controls
	LPG tank hose		Lights - Head and Tail
	Accelerator		Lights - Warning
	Alarms		Mast
	Battery Connector		Oil Leaks
	Belt		Oil Pressure
	Brakes - Parking		Overhead Guard
	Engine Oil Level		Radiator Level
	Forks		Safety Equipment
	Fuel		Steering
	Gauges		Tires
	Horn		Unusual Noises
	Hoses		Other: _____

Notes: _____
_____
_____
_____
_____
_____

Operator's Name

_____

Operator's Signature

_____

Supervisor's Name

_____

Supervisor's Signature

_____

PROPANE FORKLIFT INSPECTION CHECKLIST

Date: _____ Shift: _____

Forklift Serial Number: _____

Hour Meter Start: _____ End: _____ Total Hours: _____

	Gas gauge		Hour Meter
	LPG tank and locator pin		Hydraulic Controls
	LPG tank hose		Lights - Head and Tail
	Accelerator		Lights - Warning
	Alarms		Mast
	Battery Connector		Oil Leaks
	Belt		Oil Pressure
	Brakes - Parking		Overhead Guard
	Engine Oil Level		Radiator Level
	Forks		Safety Equipment
	Fuel		Steering
	Gauges		Tires
	Horn		Unusual Noises
	Hoses		Other: _____

Notes: _____
_____
_____
_____
_____
_____

Operator's Name

_____

Operator's Signature

_____

Supervisor's Name

_____

Supervisor's Signature

_____

PROPANE FORKLIFT INSPECTION CHECKLIST

Date: _____ Shift: _____

Forklift Serial Number: _____

Hour Meter Start: _____ End: _____ Total Hours: _____

	Gas gauge		Hour Meter
	LPG tank and locator pin		Hydraulic Controls
	LPG tank hose		Lights - Head and Tail
	Accelerator		Lights - Warning
	Alarms		Mast
	Battery Connector		Oil Leaks
	Belt		Oil Pressure
	Brakes - Parking		Overhead Guard
	Engine Oil Level		Radiator Level
	Forks		Safety Equipment
	Fuel		Steering
	Gauges		Tires
	Horn		Unusual Noises
	Hoses		Other: _____

Notes: _____
_____
_____
_____
_____
_____

Operator's Name

_____

Operator's Signature

_____

Supervisor's Name

_____

Supervisor's Signature

_____

PROPANE FORKLIFT INSPECTION CHECKLIST

Date: _____ Shift: _____

Forklift Serial Number: _____

Hour Meter Start: _____ End: _____ Total Hours: _____

Gas gauge		Hour Meter
LPG tank and locator pin		Hydraulic Controls
LPG tank hose		Lights - Head and Tail
Accelerator		Lights - Warning
Alarms		Mast
Battery Connector		Oil Leaks
Belt		Oil Pressure
Brakes - Parking		Overhead Guard
Engine Oil Level		Radiator Level
Forks		Safety Equipment
Fuel		Steering
Gauges		Tires
Horn		Unusual Noises
Hoses		Other: _____

Notes: _____
_____
_____
_____
_____
_____

Operator's Name	Supervisor's Name
_____	_____
Operator's Signature	Supervisor's Signature
_____	_____

PROPANE FORKLIFT INSPECTION CHECKLIST

Date: _____ Shift: _____

Forklift Serial Number: _____

Hour Meter Start: _____ End: _____ Total Hours: _____

	Gas gauge		Hour Meter
	LPG tank and locator pin		Hydraulic Controls
	LPG tank hose		Lights - Head and Tail
	Accelerator		Lights - Warning
	Alarms		Mast
	Battery Connector		Oil Leaks
	Belt		Oil Pressure
	Brakes - Parking		Overhead Guard
	Engine Oil Level		Radiator Level
	Forks		Safety Equipment
	Fuel		Steering
	Gauges		Tires
	Horn		Unusual Noises
	Hoses		Other: _____

Notes: _____
_____
_____
_____
_____
_____

Operator's Name	Supervisor's Name
_____	_____
Operator's Signature	Supervisor's Signature
_____	_____

PROPANE FORKLIFT INSPECTION CHECKLIST

Date: _____ Shift: _____

Forklift Serial Number: _____

Hour Meter Start: _____ End: _____ Total Hours: _____

	Gas gauge		Hour Meter
	LPG tank and locator pin		Hydraulic Controls
	LPG tank hose		Lights - Head and Tail
	Accelerator		Lights - Warning
	Alarms		Mast
	Battery Connector		Oil Leaks
	Belt		Oil Pressure
	Brakes - Parking		Overhead Guard
	Engine Oil Level		Radiator Level
	Forks		Safety Equipment
	Fuel		Steering
	Gauges		Tires
	Horn		Unusual Noises
	Hoses		Other: _____

Notes: _____
_____
_____
_____
_____
_____
_____

Operator's Name

_____

Operator's Signature

_____

Supervisor's Name

_____

Supervisor's Signature

_____

PROPANE FORKLIFT INSPECTION CHECKLIST

Date: _____ Shift: _____

Forklift Serial Number: _____

Hour Meter Start: _____ End: _____ Total Hours: _____

	Gas gauge		Hour Meter
	LPG tank and locator pin		Hydraulic Controls
	LPG tank hose		Lights - Head and Tail
	Accelerator		Lights - Warning
	Alarms		Mast
	Battery Connector		Oil Leaks
	Belt		Oil Pressure
	Brakes - Parking		Overhead Guard
	Engine Oil Level		Radiator Level
	Forks		Safety Equipment
	Fuel		Steering
	Gauges		Tires
	Horn		Unusual Noises
	Hoses		Other: _____

Notes: _____
_____
_____
_____
_____
_____

Operator's Name

_____

Operator's Signature

_____

Supervisor's Name

_____

Supervisor's Signature

_____

PROPANE FORKLIFT INSPECTION CHECKLIST

Date: _____ Shift: _____

Forklift Serial Number: _____

Hour Meter Start:_____ End:_____ Total Hours:_____

	Gas gauge		Hour Meter
	LPG tank and locator pin		Hydraulic Controls
	LPG tank hose		Lights - Head and Tail
	Accelerator		Lights - Warning
	Alarms		Mast
	Battery Connector		Oil Leaks
	Belt		Oil Pressure
	Brakes - Parking		Overhead Guard
	Engine Oil Level		Radiator Level
	Forks		Safety Equipment
	Fuel		Steering
	Gauges		Tires
	Horn		Unusual Noises
	Hoses		Other: _____

Notes: _____
_____
_____
_____
_____
_____

Operator's Name

_____

Operator's Signature

_____

Supervisor's Name

_____

Supervisor's Signature

_____

PROPANE FORKLIFT INSPECTION CHECKLIST

Date: _____ Shift: _____

Forklift Serial Number: _____

Hour Meter Start: _____ End: _____ Total Hours: _____

	Gas gauge		Hour Meter
	LPG tank and locator pin		Hydraulic Controls
	LPG tank hose		Lights - Head and Tail
	Accelerator		Lights - Warning
	Alarms		Mast
	Battery Connector		Oil Leaks
	Belt		Oil Pressure
	Brakes - Parking		Overhead Guard
	Engine Oil Level		Radiator Level
	Forks		Safety Equipment
	Fuel		Steering
	Gauges		Tires
	Horn		Unusual Noises
	Hoses		Other: _____

Notes: _____
_____
_____
_____
_____
_____

Operator's Name

_____

Operator's Signature

_____

Supervisor's Name

_____

Supervisor's Signature

_____

PROPANE FORKLIFT INSPECTION CHECKLIST

Date: _____ Shift: _____

Forklift Serial Number: _____

Hour Meter Start: _____ End: _____ Total Hours: _____

	Gas gauge		Hour Meter
	LPG tank and locator pin		Hydraulic Controls
	LPG tank hose		Lights - Head and Tail
	Accelerator		Lights - Warning
	Alarms		Mast
	Battery Connector		Oil Leaks
	Belt		Oil Pressure
	Brakes - Parking		Overhead Guard
	Engine Oil Level		Radiator Level
	Forks		Safety Equipment
	Fuel		Steering
	Gauges		Tires
	Horn		Unusual Noises
	Hoses		Other: _____

Notes: _____
_____
_____
_____
_____
_____

Operator's Name

_____

Operator's Signature

_____

Supervisor's Name

_____

Supervisor's Signature

_____

PROPANE FORKLIFT INSPECTION CHECKLIST

Date: _____ Shift: _____

Forklift Serial Number: _____

Hour Meter Start: _____ End: _____ Total Hours: _____

	Gas gauge		Hour Meter
	LPG tank and locator pin		Hydraulic Controls
	LPG tank hose		Lights - Head and Tail
	Accelerator		Lights - Warning
	Alarms		Mast
	Battery Connector		Oil Leaks
	Belt		Oil Pressure
	Brakes - Parking		Overhead Guard
	Engine Oil Level		Radiator Level
	Forks		Safety Equipment
	Fuel		Steering
	Gauges		Tires
	Horn		Unusual Noises
	Hoses		Other: _____

Notes: _____

_____

_____

_____

_____

_____

Operator's Name	Supervisor's Name
_____	_____
Operator's Signature	Supervisor's Signature
_____	_____

PROPANE FORKLIFT INSPECTION CHECKLIST

Date: _____ Shift: _____

Forklift Serial Number: _____

Hour Meter Start: _____ End: _____ Total Hours: _____

	Gas gauge		Hour Meter
	LPG tank and locator pin		Hydraulic Controls
	LPG tank hose		Lights - Head and Tail
	Accelerator		Lights - Warning
	Alarms		Mast
	Battery Connector		Oil Leaks
	Belt		Oil Pressure
	Brakes - Parking		Overhead Guard
	Engine Oil Level		Radiator Level
	Forks		Safety Equipment
	Fuel		Steering
	Gauges		Tires
	Horn		Unusual Noises
	Hoses		Other: _____

Notes: _____
_____
_____
_____
_____
_____

Operator's Name

_____

Operator's Signature

_____

Supervisor's Name

_____

Supervisor's Signature

_____

PROPANE FORKLIFT INSPECTION CHECKLIST

Date: _____ Shift: _____

Forklift Serial Number: _____

Hour Meter Start: _____ End: _____ Total Hours: _____

	Gas gauge		Hour Meter
	LPG tank and locator pin		Hydraulic Controls
	LPG tank hose		Lights - Head and Tail
	Accelerator		Lights - Warning
	Alarms		Mast
	Battery Connector		Oil Leaks
	Belt		Oil Pressure
	Brakes - Parking		Overhead Guard
	Engine Oil Level		Radiator Level
	Forks		Safety Equipment
	Fuel		Steering
	Gauges		Tires
	Horn		Unusual Noises
	Hoses		Other: _____

Notes: _____
_____
_____
_____
_____
_____

Operator's Name	Supervisor's Name
_____	_____
Operator's Signature	Supervisor's Signature
_____	_____

PROPANE FORKLIFT INSPECTION CHECKLIST

Date: _____ Shift: _____

Forklift Serial Number: _____

Hour Meter Start: _____ End: _____ Total Hours: _____

	Gas gauge		Hour Meter
	LPG tank and locator pin		Hydraulic Controls
	LPG tank hose		Lights - Head and Tail
	Accelerator		Lights - Warning
	Alarms		Mast
	Battery Connector		Oil Leaks
	Belt		Oil Pressure
	Brakes - Parking		Overhead Guard
	Engine Oil Level		Radiator Level
	Forks		Safety Equipment
	Fuel		Steering
	Gauges		Tires
	Horn		Unusual Noises
	Hoses		Other: _____

Notes: _____
_____
_____
_____
_____
_____
_____

Operator's Name	Supervisor's Name
_____	_____
Operator's Signature	Supervisor's Signature
_____	_____

PROPANE FORKLIFT INSPECTION CHECKLIST

Date: _____ Shift: _____

Forklift Serial Number: _____

Hour Meter Start: _____ End: _____ Total Hours: _____

	Gas gauge		Hour Meter
	LPG tank and locator pin		Hydraulic Controls
	LPG tank hose		Lights - Head and Tail
	Accelerator		Lights - Warning
	Alarms		Mast
	Battery Connector		Oil Leaks
	Belt		Oil Pressure
	Brakes - Parking		Overhead Guard
	Engine Oil Level		Radiator Level
	Forks		Safety Equipment
	Fuel		Steering
	Gauges		Tires
	Horn		Unusual Noises
	Hoses		Other: _____

Notes: _____
_____
_____
_____
_____
_____

Operator's Name	Supervisor's Name
_____	_____
Operator's Signature	Supervisor's Signature
_____	_____

PROPANE FORKLIFT INSPECTION CHECKLIST

Date: _____ Shift: _____

Forklift Serial Number: _____

Hour Meter Start: _____ End: _____ Total Hours: _____

	Gas gauge		Hour Meter
	LPG tank and locator pin		Hydraulic Controls
	LPG tank hose		Lights - Head and Tail
	Accelerator		Lights - Warning
	Alarms		Mast
	Battery Connector		Oil Leaks
	Belt		Oil Pressure
	Brakes - Parking		Overhead Guard
	Engine Oil Level		Radiator Level
	Forks		Safety Equipment
	Fuel		Steering
	Gauges		Tires
	Horn		Unusual Noises
	Hoses		Other: _____

Notes: _____
_____
_____
_____
_____
_____

Operator's Name	Supervisor's Name
_____	_____
Operator's Signature	Supervisor's Signature
_____	_____

PROPANE FORKLIFT INSPECTION CHECKLIST

Date: _____ Shift: _____

Forklift Serial Number: _____

Hour Meter Start: _____ End: _____ Total Hours: _____

	Gas gauge		Hour Meter
	LPG tank and locator pin		Hydraulic Controls
	LPG tank hose		Lights - Head and Tail
	Accelerator		Lights - Warning
	Alarms		Mast
	Battery Connector		Oil Leaks
	Belt		Oil Pressure
	Brakes - Parking		Overhead Guard
	Engine Oil Level		Radiator Level
	Forks		Safety Equipment
	Fuel		Steering
	Gauges		Tires
	Horn		Unusual Noises
	Hoses		Other: _____

Notes: _____
_____
_____
_____
_____
_____

Operator's Name	Supervisor's Name
_____	_____
Operator's Signature	Supervisor's Signature
_____	_____

PROPANE FORKLIFT INSPECTION CHECKLIST

Date: _____ Shift: _____

Forklift Serial Number: _____

Hour Meter Start: _____ End: _____ Total Hours: _____

	Gas gauge		Hour Meter
	LPG tank and locator pin		Hydraulic Controls
	LPG tank hose		Lights - Head and Tail
	Accelerator		Lights - Warning
	Alarms		Mast
	Battery Connector		Oil Leaks
	Belt		Oil Pressure
	Brakes - Parking		Overhead Guard
	Engine Oil Level		Radiator Level
	Forks		Safety Equipment
	Fuel		Steering
	Gauges		Tires
	Horn		Unusual Noises
	Hoses		Other: _____

Notes: _____
_____
_____
_____
_____
_____

Operator's Name

_____

Operator's Signature

_____

Supervisor's Name

_____

Supervisor's Signature

_____

PROPANE FORKLIFT INSPECTION CHECKLIST

Date: _____ Shift: _____

Forklift Serial Number: _____

Hour Meter Start: _____ End: _____ Total Hours: _____

Gas gauge		Hour Meter
LPG tank and locator pin		Hydraulic Controls
LPG tank hose		Lights - Head and Tail
Accelerator		Lights - Warning
Alarms		Mast
Battery Connector		Oil Leaks
Belt		Oil Pressure
Brakes - Parking		Overhead Guard
Engine Oil Level		Radiator Level
Forks		Safety Equipment
Fuel		Steering
Gauges		Tires
Horn		Unusual Noises
Hoses		Other: _____

Notes: _____
_____
_____
_____
_____
_____

Operator's Name	Supervisor's Name
_____	_____
Operator's Signature	Supervisor's Signature
_____	_____

PROPANE FORKLIFT INSPECTION CHECKLIST

Date: _____ Shift: _____

Forklift Serial Number: _____

Hour Meter Start: _____ End: _____ Total Hours: _____

Gas gauge		Hour Meter
LPG tank and locator pin		Hydraulic Controls
LPG tank hose		Lights - Head and Tail
Accelerator		Lights - Warning
Alarms		Mast
Battery Connector		Oil Leaks
Belt		Oil Pressure
Brakes - Parking		Overhead Guard
Engine Oil Level		Radiator Level
Forks		Safety Equipment
Fuel		Steering
Gauges		Tires
Horn		Unusual Noises
Hoses		Other: _____

Notes: _____

_____

_____

_____

_____

_____

Operator's Name	Supervisor's Name
_____	_____
Operator's Signature	Supervisor's Signature
_____	_____

PROPANE FORKLIFT INSPECTION CHECKLIST

Date: _____ Shift: _____

Forklift Serial Number: _____

Hour Meter Start: _____ End: _____ Total Hours: _____

	Gas gauge		Hour Meter
	LPG tank and locator pin		Hydraulic Controls
	LPG tank hose		Lights - Head and Tail
	Accelerator		Lights - Warning
	Alarms		Mast
	Battery Connector		Oil Leaks
	Belt		Oil Pressure
	Brakes - Parking		Overhead Guard
	Engine Oil Level		Radiator Level
	Forks		Safety Equipment
	Fuel		Steering
	Gauges		Tires
	Horn		Unusual Noises
	Hoses		Other: _____

Notes: _____
_____
_____
_____
_____
_____

Operator's Name
_____

Operator's Signature
_____

Supervisor's Name
_____

Supervisor's Signature
_____

PROPANE FORKLIFT INSPECTION CHECKLIST

Date: _____ Shift: _____

Forklift Serial Number: _____

Hour Meter Start: _____ End: _____ Total Hours: _____

	Gas gauge		Hour Meter
	LPG tank and locator pin		Hydraulic Controls
	LPG tank hose		Lights - Head and Tail
	Accelerator		Lights - Warning
	Alarms		Mast
	Battery Connector		Oil Leaks
	Belt		Oil Pressure
	Brakes - Parking		Overhead Guard
	Engine Oil Level		Radiator Level
	Forks		Safety Equipment
	Fuel		Steering
	Gauges		Tires
	Horn		Unusual Noises
	Hoses		Other: _____

Notes: _____
_____
_____
_____
_____
_____

Operator's Name

_____

Operator's Signature

_____

Supervisor's Name

_____

Supervisor's Signature

_____

PROPANE FORKLIFT INSPECTION CHECKLIST

Date: _____ Shift: _____

Forklift Serial Number: _____

Hour Meter Start: _____ End: _____ Total Hours: _____

	Gas gauge			Hour Meter
	LPG tank and locator pin			Hydraulic Controls
	LPG tank hose			Lights - Head and Tail
	Accelerator			Lights - Warning
	Alarms			Mast
	Battery Connector			Oil Leaks
	Belt			Oil Pressure
	Brakes - Parking			Overhead Guard
	Engine Oil Level			Radiator Level
	Forks			Safety Equipment
	Fuel			Steering
	Gauges			Tires
	Horn			Unusual Noises
	Hoses			Other: _____

Notes: _____
_____
_____
_____
_____
_____

Operator's Name	Supervisor's Name
_____	_____
Operator's Signature	Supervisor's Signature
_____	_____

PROPANE FORKLIFT INSPECTION CHECKLIST

Date: _____ Shift: _____

Forklift Serial Number: _____

Hour Meter Start: _____ End: _____ Total Hours: _____

Gas gauge		Hour Meter
LPG tank and locator pin		Hydraulic Controls
LPG tank hose		Lights - Head and Tail
Accelerator		Lights - Warning
Alarms		Mast
Battery Connector		Oil Leaks
Belt		Oil Pressure
Brakes - Parking		Overhead Guard
Engine Oil Level		Radiator Level
Forks		Safety Equipment
Fuel		Steering
Gauges		Tires
Horn		Unusual Noises
Hoses		Other: _____

Notes: _____
_____
_____
_____
_____
_____

Operator's Name

_____

Operator's Signature

_____

Supervisor's Name

_____

Supervisor's Signature

_____

PROPANE FORKLIFT INSPECTION CHECKLIST

Date: _____ Shift: _____

Forklift Serial Number: _____

Hour Meter Start: _____ End: _____ Total Hours: _____

	Gas gauge		Hour Meter
	LPG tank and locator pin		Hydraulic Controls
	LPG tank hose		Lights - Head and Tail
	Accelerator		Lights - Warning
	Alarms		Mast
	Battery Connector		Oil Leaks
	Belt		Oil Pressure
	Brakes - Parking		Overhead Guard
	Engine Oil Level		Radiator Level
	Forks		Safety Equipment
	Fuel		Steering
	Gauges		Tires
	Horn		Unusual Noises
	Hoses		Other: _____

Notes: _____
_____
_____
_____
_____
_____

Operator's Name

_____

Operator's Signature

_____

Supervisor's Name

_____

Supervisor's Signature

_____

PROPANE FORKLIFT INSPECTION CHECKLIST

Date: _____ Shift: _____

Forklift Serial Number: _____

Hour Meter Start: _____ End: _____ Total Hours: _____

Gas gauge		Hour Meter	
LPG tank and locator pin		Hydraulic Controls	
LPG tank hose		Lights - Head and Tail	
Accelerator		Lights - Warning	
Alarms		Mast	
Battery Connector		Oil Leaks	
Belt		Oil Pressure	
Brakes - Parking		Overhead Guard	
Engine Oil Level		Radiator Level	
Forks		Safety Equipment	
Fuel		Steering	
Gauges		Tires	
Horn		Unusual Noises	
Hoses		Other: _____	

Notes: _____
_____
_____
_____
_____
_____

Operator's Name

_____

Operator's Signature

_____

Supervisor's Name

_____

Supervisor's Signature

_____

PROPANE FORKLIFT INSPECTION CHECKLIST

Date: _____ Shift: _____

Forklift Serial Number: _____

Hour Meter Start: _____ End: _____ Total Hours: _____

	Gas gauge		Hour Meter
	LPG tank and locator pin		Hydraulic Controls
	LPG tank hose		Lights - Head and Tail
	Accelerator		Lights - Warning
	Alarms		Mast
	Battery Connector		Oil Leaks
	Belt		Oil Pressure
	Brakes - Parking		Overhead Guard
	Engine Oil Level		Radiator Level
	Forks		Safety Equipment
	Fuel		Steering
	Gauges		Tires
	Horn		Unusual Noises
	Hoses		Other: _____

Notes: _____
_____
_____
_____
_____
_____

Operator's Name	Supervisor's Name
_____	_____
Operator's Signature	Supervisor's Signature
_____	_____

PROPANE FORKLIFT INSPECTION CHECKLIST

Date: _____ Shift: _____

Forklift Serial Number: _____

Hour Meter Start:_____ End:_____ Total Hours:_____

	Gas gauge		Hour Meter
	LPG tank and locator pin		Hydraulic Controls
	LPG tank hose		Lights - Head and Tail
	Accelerator		Lights - Warning
	Alarms		Mast
	Battery Connector		Oil Leaks
	Belt		Oil Pressure
	Brakes - Parking		Overhead Guard
	Engine Oil Level		Radiator Level
	Forks		Safety Equipment
	Fuel		Steering
	Gauges		Tires
	Horn		Unusual Noises
	Hoses		Other: _____

Notes: _____
_____
_____
_____
_____
_____

Operator's Name	Supervisor's Name
_____	_____
Operator's Signature	Supervisor's Signature
_____	_____

PROPANE FORKLIFT INSPECTION CHECKLIST

Date: _____ Shift: _____

Forklift Serial Number: _____

Hour Meter Start: _____ End: _____ Total Hours: _____

	Gas gauge		Hour Meter
	LPG tank and locator pin		Hydraulic Controls
	LPG tank hose		Lights - Head and Tail
	Accelerator		Lights - Warning
	Alarms		Mast
	Battery Connector		Oil Leaks
	Belt		Oil Pressure
	Brakes - Parking		Overhead Guard
	Engine Oil Level		Radiator Level
	Forks		Safety Equipment
	Fuel		Steering
	Gauges		Tires
	Horn		Unusual Noises
	Hoses		Other: _____

Notes: _____
_____
_____
_____
_____
_____

Operator's Name	Supervisor's Name
Operator's Signature	Supervisor's Signature

PROPANE FORKLIFT INSPECTION CHECKLIST

Date: _____ Shift: _____

Forklift Serial Number: _____

Hour Meter Start: _____ End: _____ Total Hours: _____

	Gas gauge		Hour Meter
	LPG tank and locator pin		Hydraulic Controls
	LPG tank hose		Lights - Head and Tail
	Accelerator		Lights - Warning
	Alarms		Mast
	Battery Connector		Oil Leaks
	Belt		Oil Pressure
	Brakes - Parking		Overhead Guard
	Engine Oil Level		Radiator Level
	Forks		Safety Equipment
	Fuel		Steering
	Gauges		Tires
	Horn		Unusual Noises
	Hoses		Other: _____

Notes: _____
_____
_____
_____
_____
_____

Operator's Name

_____

Operator's Signature

_____

Supervisor's Name

_____

Supervisor's Signature

_____

PROPANE FORKLIFT INSPECTION CHECKLIST

Date: _____ Shift: _____

Forklift Serial Number: _____

Hour Meter Start: _____ End: _____ Total Hours: _____

	Gas gauge		Hour Meter	
	LPG tank and locator pin		Hydraulic Controls	
	LPG tank hose		Lights - Head and Tail	
	Accelerator		Lights - Warning	
	Alarms		Mast	
	Battery Connector		Oil Leaks	
	Belt		Oil Pressure	
	Brakes - Parking		Overhead Guard	
	Engine Oil Level		Radiator Level	
	Forks		Safety Equipment	
	Fuel		Steering	
	Gauges		Tires	
	Horn		Unusual Noises	
	Hoses		Other: _____	

Notes: _____
_____
_____
_____
_____
_____

Operator's Name

_____

Operator's Signature

_____

Supervisor's Name

_____

Supervisor's Signature

_____

PROPANE FORKLIFT INSPECTION CHECKLIST

Date: _____ Shift: _____

Forklift Serial Number: _____

Hour Meter Start: _____ End: _____ Total Hours: _____

	Gas gauge		Hour Meter
	LPG tank and locator pin		Hydraulic Controls
	LPG tank hose		Lights - Head and Tail
	Accelerator		Lights - Warning
	Alarms		Mast
	Battery Connector		Oil Leaks
	Belt		Oil Pressure
	Brakes - Parking		Overhead Guard
	Engine Oil Level		Radiator Level
	Forks		Safety Equipment
	Fuel		Steering
	Gauges		Tires
	Horn		Unusual Noises
	Hoses		Other: _____

Notes: _____
_____
_____
_____
_____
_____

Operator's Name
_____

Operator's Signature
_____

Supervisor's Name
_____

Supervisor's Signature
_____

PROPANE FORKLIFT INSPECTION CHECKLIST

Date: _____ Shift: _____

Forklift Serial Number: _____

Hour Meter Start: _____ End: _____ Total Hours: _____

	Gas gauge			Hour Meter
	LPG tank and locator pin			Hydraulic Controls
	LPG tank hose			Lights - Head and Tail
	Accelerator			Lights - Warning
	Alarms			Mast
	Battery Connector			Oil Leaks
	Belt			Oil Pressure
	Brakes - Parking			Overhead Guard
	Engine Oil Level			Radiator Level
	Forks			Safety Equipment
	Fuel			Steering
	Gauges			Tires
	Horn			Unusual Noises
	Hoses			Other: _____

Notes: _____

_____

_____

_____

_____

_____

Operator's Name

_____

Operator's Signature

_____

Supervisor's Name

_____

Supervisor's Signature

_____

PROPANE FORKLIFT INSPECTION CHECKLIST

Date: _____ Shift: _____

Forklift Serial Number: _____

Hour Meter Start: _____ End: _____ Total Hours: _____

	Gas gauge		Hour Meter
	LPG tank and locator pin		Hydraulic Controls
	LPG tank hose		Lights - Head and Tail
	Accelerator		Lights - Warning
	Alarms		Mast
	Battery Connector		Oil Leaks
	Belt		Oil Pressure
	Brakes - Parking		Overhead Guard
	Engine Oil Level		Radiator Level
	Forks		Safety Equipment
	Fuel		Steering
	Gauges		Tires
	Horn		Unusual Noises
	Hoses		Other: _____

Notes: _____
_____
_____
_____
_____
_____

Operator's Name	Supervisor's Name
_____	_____
Operator's Signature	Supervisor's Signature
_____	_____

PROPANE FORKLIFT INSPECTION CHECKLIST

Date: _____ Shift: _____

Forklift Serial Number: _____

Hour Meter Start: _____ End: _____ Total Hours: _____

	Gas gauge		Hour Meter
	LPG tank and locator pin		Hydraulic Controls
	LPG tank hose		Lights - Head and Tail
	Accelerator		Lights - Warning
	Alarms		Mast
	Battery Connector		Oil Leaks
	Belt		Oil Pressure
	Brakes - Parking		Overhead Guard
	Engine Oil Level		Radiator Level
	Forks		Safety Equipment
	Fuel		Steering
	Gauges		Tires
	Horn		Unusual Noises
	Hoses		Other: _____

Notes: _____
_____
_____
_____
_____
_____

Operator's Name	Supervisor's Name
_____	_____
Operator's Signature	Supervisor's Signature
_____	_____

PROPANE FORKLIFT INSPECTION CHECKLIST

Date: _____ Shift: _____

Forklift Serial Number: _____

Hour Meter Start: _____ End: _____ Total Hours: _____

	Gas gauge		Hour Meter
	LPG tank and locator pin		Hydraulic Controls
	LPG tank hose		Lights - Head and Tail
	Accelerator		Lights - Warning
	Alarms		Mast
	Battery Connector		Oil Leaks
	Belt		Oil Pressure
	Brakes - Parking		Overhead Guard
	Engine Oil Level		Radiator Level
	Forks		Safety Equipment
	Fuel		Steering
	Gauges		Tires
	Horn		Unusual Noises
	Hoses		Other: _____

Notes: _____

_____

_____

_____

_____

_____

Operator's Name

_____

Operator's Signature

_____

Supervisor's Name

_____

Supervisor's Signature

_____

PROPANE FORKLIFT INSPECTION CHECKLIST

Date: _____ Shift: _____

Forklift Serial Number: _____

Hour Meter Start: _____ End: _____ Total Hours: _____

	Gas gauge		Hour Meter
	LPG tank and locator pin		Hydraulic Controls
	LPG tank hose		Lights - Head and Tail
	Accelerator		Lights - Warning
	Alarms		Mast
	Battery Connector		Oil Leaks
	Belt		Oil Pressure
	Brakes - Parking		Overhead Guard
	Engine Oil Level		Radiator Level
	Forks		Safety Equipment
	Fuel		Steering
	Gauges		Tires
	Horn		Unusual Noises
	Hoses		Other: _____

Notes: _____
_____
_____
_____
_____
_____

Operator's Name

_____

Operator's Signature

_____

Supervisor's Name

_____

Supervisor's Signature

_____

PROPANE FORKLIFT INSPECTION CHECKLIST

Date: _____ Shift: _____

Forklift Serial Number: _____

Hour Meter Start: _____ End: _____ Total Hours: _____

	Gas gauge		Hour Meter
	LPG tank and locator pin		Hydraulic Controls
	LPG tank hose		Lights - Head and Tail
	Accelerator		Lights - Warning
	Alarms		Mast
	Battery Connector		Oil Leaks
	Belt		Oil Pressure
	Brakes - Parking		Overhead Guard
	Engine Oil Level		Radiator Level
	Forks		Safety Equipment
	Fuel		Steering
	Gauges		Tires
	Horn		Unusual Noises
	Hoses		Other: _____

Notes: _____
_____
_____
_____
_____
_____
_____

Operator's Name	Supervisor's Name
_____	_____
Operator's Signature	Supervisor's Signature
_____	_____

PROPANE FORKLIFT INSPECTION CHECKLIST

Date: _____ Shift: _____

Forklift Serial Number: _____

Hour Meter Start: _____ End: _____ Total Hours: _____

	Gas gauge		Hour Meter
	LPG tank and locator pin		Hydraulic Controls
	LPG tank hose		Lights - Head and Tail
	Accelerator		Lights - Warning
	Alarms		Mast
	Battery Connector		Oil Leaks
	Belt		Oil Pressure
	Brakes - Parking		Overhead Guard
	Engine Oil Level		Radiator Level
	Forks		Safety Equipment
	Fuel		Steering
	Gauges		Tires
	Horn		Unusual Noises
	Hoses		Other: _____

Notes: _____

_____

_____

_____

_____

_____

Operator's Name	Supervisor's Name
Operator's Signature	Supervisor's Signature

PROPANE FORKLIFT INSPECTION CHECKLIST

Date: _____ Shift: _____

Forklift Serial Number: _____

Hour Meter Start: _____ End: _____ Total Hours: _____

	Gas gauge		Hour Meter
	LPG tank and locator pin		Hydraulic Controls
	LPG tank hose		Lights - Head and Tail
	Accelerator		Lights - Warning
	Alarms		Mast
	Battery Connector		Oil Leaks
	Belt		Oil Pressure
	Brakes - Parking		Overhead Guard
	Engine Oil Level		Radiator Level
	Forks		Safety Equipment
	Fuel		Steering
	Gauges		Tires
	Horn		Unusual Noises
	Hoses		Other: _____

Notes: _____
_____
_____
_____
_____
_____
_____

Operator's Name	Supervisor's Name
_____	_____
Operator's Signature	Supervisor's Signature
_____	_____

PROPANE FORKLIFT INSPECTION CHECKLIST

Date: _____ Shift: _____

Forklift Serial Number: _____

Hour Meter Start: _____ End: _____ Total Hours: _____

	Gas gauge		Hour Meter
	LPG tank and locator pin		Hydraulic Controls
	LPG tank hose		Lights - Head and Tail
	Accelerator		Lights - Warning
	Alarms		Mast
	Battery Connector		Oil Leaks
	Belt		Oil Pressure
	Brakes - Parking		Overhead Guard
	Engine Oil Level		Radiator Level
	Forks		Safety Equipment
	Fuel		Steering
	Gauges		Tires
	Horn		Unusual Noises
	Hoses		Other: _____

Notes: _____
_____
_____
_____
_____
_____

Operator's Name	Supervisor's Name
_____	_____
Operator's Signature	Supervisor's Signature
_____	_____

PROPANE FORKLIFT INSPECTION CHECKLIST

Date: _____ Shift: _____

Forklift Serial Number: _____

Hour Meter Start: _____ End: _____ Total Hours: _____

	Gas gauge		Hour Meter
	LPG tank and locator pin		Hydraulic Controls
	LPG tank hose		Lights - Head and Tail
	Accelerator		Lights - Warning
	Alarms		Mast
	Battery Connector		Oil Leaks
	Belt		Oil Pressure
	Brakes - Parking		Overhead Guard
	Engine Oil Level		Radiator Level
	Forks		Safety Equipment
	Fuel		Steering
	Gauges		Tires
	Horn		Unusual Noises
	Hoses		Other: _____

Notes: _____

_____

_____

_____

_____

_____

Operator's Name	Supervisor's Name
_____	_____
Operator's Signature	Supervisor's Signature
_____	_____

PROPANE FORKLIFT INSPECTION CHECKLIST

Date: _____ Shift: _____

Forklift Serial Number: _____

Hour Meter Start: _____ End: _____ Total Hours: _____

	Gas gauge		Hour Meter
	LPG tank and locator pin		Hydraulic Controls
	LPG tank hose		Lights - Head and Tail
	Accelerator		Lights - Warning
	Alarms		Mast
	Battery Connector		Oil Leaks
	Belt		Oil Pressure
	Brakes - Parking		Overhead Guard
	Engine Oil Level		Radiator Level
	Forks		Safety Equipment
	Fuel		Steering
	Gauges		Tires
	Horn		Unusual Noises
	Hoses		Other: _____

Notes: _____

_____

_____

_____

_____

_____

Operator's Name	Supervisor's Name
_____	_____
Operator's Signature	Supervisor's Signature
_____	_____

PROPANE FORKLIFT INSPECTION CHECKLIST

Date: _____ Shift: _____

Forklift Serial Number: _____

Hour Meter Start: _____ End: _____ Total Hours: _____

	Gas gauge		Hour Meter
	LPG tank and locator pin		Hydraulic Controls
	LPG tank hose		Lights - Head and Tail
	Accelerator		Lights - Warning
	Alarms		Mast
	Battery Connector		Oil Leaks
	Belt		Oil Pressure
	Brakes - Parking		Overhead Guard
	Engine Oil Level		Radiator Level
	Forks		Safety Equipment
	Fuel		Steering
	Gauges		Tires
	Horn		Unusual Noises
	Hoses		Other: _____

Notes: _____
_____
_____
_____
_____
_____
_____

Operator's Name

_____

Operator's Signature

_____

Supervisor's Name

_____

Supervisor's Signature

_____

PROPANE FORKLIFT INSPECTION CHECKLIST

Date: _____ Shift: _____

Forklift Serial Number: _____

Hour Meter Start: _____ End: _____ Total Hours: _____

	Gas gauge		Hour Meter
	LPG tank and locator pin		Hydraulic Controls
	LPG tank hose		Lights - Head and Tail
	Accelerator		Lights - Warning
	Alarms		Mast
	Battery Connector		Oil Leaks
	Belt		Oil Pressure
	Brakes - Parking		Overhead Guard
	Engine Oil Level		Radiator Level
	Forks		Safety Equipment
	Fuel		Steering
	Gauges		Tires
	Horn		Unusual Noises
	Hoses		Other: _____

Notes: _____
_____
_____
_____
_____
_____

Operator's Name

_____

Operator's Signature

_____

Supervisor's Name

_____

Supervisor's Signature

_____

PROPANE FORKLIFT INSPECTION CHECKLIST

Date: _____ Shift: _____

Forklift Serial Number: _____

Hour Meter Start: _____ End: _____ Total Hours: _____

	Gas gauge		Hour Meter
	LPG tank and locator pin		Hydraulic Controls
	LPG tank hose		Lights - Head and Tail
	Accelerator		Lights - Warning
	Alarms		Mast
	Battery Connector		Oil Leaks
	Belt		Oil Pressure
	Brakes - Parking		Overhead Guard
	Engine Oil Level		Radiator Level
	Forks		Safety Equipment
	Fuel		Steering
	Gauges		Tires
	Horn		Unusual Noises
	Hoses		Other: _____

Notes: _____

_____

_____

_____

_____

_____

Operator's Name	Supervisor's Name
_____	_____
Operator's Signature	Supervisor's Signature
_____	_____

PROPANE FORKLIFT INSPECTION CHECKLIST

Date: _____ Shift: _____

Forklift Serial Number: _____

Hour Meter Start: _____ End: _____ Total Hours: _____

	Gas gauge		Hour Meter
	LPG tank and locator pin		Hydraulic Controls
	LPG tank hose		Lights - Head and Tail
	Accelerator		Lights - Warning
	Alarms		Mast
	Battery Connector		Oil Leaks
	Belt		Oil Pressure
	Brakes - Parking		Overhead Guard
	Engine Oil Level		Radiator Level
	Forks		Safety Equipment
	Fuel		Steering
	Gauges		Tires
	Horn		Unusual Noises
	Hoses		Other: _____

Notes: _____
_____
_____
_____
_____
_____

Operator's Name	Supervisor's Name
_____	_____
Operator's Signature	Supervisor's Signature
_____	_____

PROPANE FORKLIFT INSPECTION CHECKLIST

Date: _____ Shift: _____

Forklift Serial Number: _____

Hour Meter Start: _____ End: _____ Total Hours: _____

	Gas gauge		Hour Meter
	LPG tank and locator pin		Hydraulic Controls
	LPG tank hose		Lights - Head and Tail
	Accelerator		Lights - Warning
	Alarms		Mast
	Battery Connector		Oil Leaks
	Belt		Oil Pressure
	Brakes - Parking		Overhead Guard
	Engine Oil Level		Radiator Level
	Forks		Safety Equipment
	Fuel		Steering
	Gauges		Tires
	Horn		Unusual Noises
	Hoses		Other: _____

Notes: _____
_____
_____
_____
_____
_____

Operator's Name	Supervisor's Name
_____	_____
Operator's Signature	Supervisor's Signature
_____	_____

PROPANE FORKLIFT INSPECTION CHECKLIST

Date: _____ Shift: _____

Forklift Serial Number: _____

Hour Meter Start: _____ End: _____ Total Hours: _____

Gas gauge		Hour Meter	
LPG tank and locator pin		Hydraulic Controls	
LPG tank hose		Lights - Head and Tail	
Accelerator		Lights - Warning	
Alarms		Mast	
Battery Connector		Oil Leaks	
Belt		Oil Pressure	
Brakes - Parking		Overhead Guard	
Engine Oil Level		Radiator Level	
Forks		Safety Equipment	
Fuel		Steering	
Gauges		Tires	
Horn		Unusual Noises	
Hoses		Other: _____	

Notes: _____
_____
_____
_____
_____
_____

Operator's Name

_____

Operator's Signature

_____

Supervisor's Name

_____

Supervisor's Signature

_____

PROPANE FORKLIFT INSPECTION CHECKLIST

Date: _____ Shift: _____

Forklift Serial Number: _____

Hour Meter Start: _____ End: _____ Total Hours: _____

Gas gauge		Hour Meter	
LPG tank and locator pin		Hydraulic Controls	
LPG tank hose		Lights - Head and Tail	
Accelerator		Lights - Warning	
Alarms		Mast	
Battery Connector		Oil Leaks	
Belt		Oil Pressure	
Brakes - Parking		Overhead Guard	
Engine Oil Level		Radiator Level	
Forks		Safety Equipment	
Fuel		Steering	
Gauges		Tires	
Horn		Unusual Noises	
Hoses		Other: _____	

Notes: _____
_____
_____
_____
_____
_____

Operator's Name	Supervisor's Name
_____	_____
Operator's Signature	Supervisor's Signature
_____	_____

PROPANE FORKLIFT INSPECTION CHECKLIST

Date: _____ Shift: _____

Forklift Serial Number: _____

Hour Meter Start: _____ End: _____ Total Hours: _____

	Gas gauge		Hour Meter
	LPG tank and locator pin		Hydraulic Controls
	LPG tank hose		Lights - Head and Tail
	Accelerator		Lights - Warning
	Alarms		Mast
	Battery Connector		Oil Leaks
	Belt		Oil Pressure
	Brakes - Parking		Overhead Guard
	Engine Oil Level		Radiator Level
	Forks		Safety Equipment
	Fuel		Steering
	Gauges		Tires
	Horn		Unusual Noises
	Hoses		Other: _____

Notes: _____
_____
_____
_____
_____
_____

Operator's Name	Supervisor's Name
_____	_____
Operator's Signature	Supervisor's Signature
_____	_____

PROPANE FORKLIFT INSPECTION CHECKLIST

Date: _____ Shift: _____

Forklift Serial Number: _____

Hour Meter Start: _____ End: _____ Total Hours: _____

	Gas gauge		Hour Meter
	LPG tank and locator pin		Hydraulic Controls
	LPG tank hose		Lights - Head and Tail
	Accelerator		Lights - Warning
	Alarms		Mast
	Battery Connector		Oil Leaks
	Belt		Oil Pressure
	Brakes - Parking		Overhead Guard
	Engine Oil Level		Radiator Level
	Forks		Safety Equipment
	Fuel		Steering
	Gauges		Tires
	Horn		Unusual Noises
	Hoses		Other: _____

Notes: _____
_____
_____
_____
_____
_____

Operator's Name

_____

Operator's Signature

_____

Supervisor's Name

_____

Supervisor's Signature

_____

PROPANE FORKLIFT INSPECTION CHECKLIST

Date: _____ Shift: _____

Forklift Serial Number: _____

Hour Meter Start: _____ End: _____ Total Hours: _____

	Gas gauge		Hour Meter
	LPG tank and locator pin		Hydraulic Controls
	LPG tank hose		Lights - Head and Tail
	Accelerator		Lights - Warning
	Alarms		Mast
	Battery Connector		Oil Leaks
	Belt		Oil Pressure
	Brakes - Parking		Overhead Guard
	Engine Oil Level		Radiator Level
	Forks		Safety Equipment
	Fuel		Steering
	Gauges		Tires
	Horn		Unusual Noises
	Hoses		Other: _____

Notes: _____
_____
_____
_____
_____
_____

Operator's Name	Supervisor's Name
_____	_____
Operator's Signature	Supervisor's Signature
_____	_____

PROPANE FORKLIFT INSPECTION CHECKLIST

Date: _____ Shift: _____

Forklift Serial Number: _____

Hour Meter Start: _____ End: _____ Total Hours: _____

	Gas gauge		Hour Meter
	LPG tank and locator pin		Hydraulic Controls
	LPG tank hose		Lights - Head and Tail
	Accelerator		Lights - Warning
	Alarms		Mast
	Battery Connector		Oil Leaks
	Belt		Oil Pressure
	Brakes - Parking		Overhead Guard
	Engine Oil Level		Radiator Level
	Forks		Safety Equipment
	Fuel		Steering
	Gauges		Tires
	Horn		Unusual Noises
	Hoses		Other: _____

Notes: _____
_____
_____
_____
_____
_____

Operator's Name	Supervisor's Name
_____	_____
Operator's Signature	Supervisor's Signature
_____	_____

PROPANE FORKLIFT INSPECTION CHECKLIST

Date: _____ Shift: _____

Forklift Serial Number: _____

Hour Meter Start: _____ End: _____ Total Hours: _____

	Gas gauge		Hour Meter
	LPG tank and locator pin		Hydraulic Controls
	LPG tank hose		Lights - Head and Tail
	Accelerator		Lights - Warning
	Alarms		Mast
	Battery Connector		Oil Leaks
	Belt		Oil Pressure
	Brakes - Parking		Overhead Guard
	Engine Oil Level		Radiator Level
	Forks		Safety Equipment
	Fuel		Steering
	Gauges		Tires
	Horn		Unusual Noises
	Hoses		Other: _____

Notes: _____
_____
_____
_____
_____
_____

Operator's Name	Supervisor's Name
_____	_____
Operator's Signature	Supervisor's Signature
_____	_____

PROPANE FORKLIFT INSPECTION CHECKLIST

Date: _____ Shift: _____

Forklift Serial Number: _____

Hour Meter Start: _____ End: _____ Total Hours: _____

	Gas gauge		Hour Meter
	LPG tank and locator pin		Hydraulic Controls
	LPG tank hose		Lights - Head and Tail
	Accelerator		Lights - Warning
	Alarms		Mast
	Battery Connector		Oil Leaks
	Belt		Oil Pressure
	Brakes - Parking		Overhead Guard
	Engine Oil Level		Radiator Level
	Forks		Safety Equipment
	Fuel		Steering
	Gauges		Tires
	Horn		Unusual Noises
	Hoses		Other: _____

Notes: _____
_____
_____
_____
_____
_____

Operator's Name	Supervisor's Name
_____	_____
Operator's Signature	Supervisor's Signature
_____	_____

PROPANE FORKLIFT INSPECTION CHECKLIST

Date: _____ Shift: _____

Forklift Serial Number: _____

Hour Meter Start: _____ End: _____ Total Hours: _____

	Gas gauge		Hour Meter
	LPG tank and locator pin		Hydraulic Controls
	LPG tank hose		Lights - Head and Tail
	Accelerator		Lights - Warning
	Alarms		Mast
	Battery Connector		Oil Leaks
	Belt		Oil Pressure
	Brakes - Parking		Overhead Guard
	Engine Oil Level		Radiator Level
	Forks		Safety Equipment
	Fuel		Steering
	Gauges		Tires
	Horn		Unusual Noises
	Hoses		Other: _____

Notes: _____
_____
_____
_____
_____
_____

Operator's Name

_____

Operator's Signature

_____

Supervisor's Name

_____

Supervisor's Signature

_____

PROPANE FORKLIFT INSPECTION CHECKLIST

Date: _____ Shift: _____

Forklift Serial Number: _____

Hour Meter Start: _____ End: _____ Total Hours: _____

	Gas gauge		Hour Meter
	LPG tank and locator pin		Hydraulic Controls
	LPG tank hose		Lights - Head and Tail
	Accelerator		Lights - Warning
	Alarms		Mast
	Battery Connector		Oil Leaks
	Belt		Oil Pressure
	Brakes - Parking		Overhead Guard
	Engine Oil Level		Radiator Level
	Forks		Safety Equipment
	Fuel		Steering
	Gauges		Tires
	Horn		Unusual Noises
	Hoses		Other: _____

Notes: _____
_____
_____
_____
_____
_____

Operator's Name	Supervisor's Name
_____	_____
Operator's Signature	Supervisor's Signature
_____	_____

PROPANE FORKLIFT INSPECTION CHECKLIST

Date: _____ Shift: _____

Forklift Serial Number: _____

Hour Meter Start: _____ End: _____ Total Hours: _____

	Gas gauge			Hour Meter
	LPG tank and locator pin			Hydraulic Controls
	LPG tank hose			Lights - Head and Tail
	Accelerator			Lights - Warning
	Alarms			Mast
	Battery Connector			Oil Leaks
	Belt			Oil Pressure
	Brakes - Parking			Overhead Guard
	Engine Oil Level			Radiator Level
	Forks			Safety Equipment
	Fuel			Steering
	Gauges			Tires
	Horn			Unusual Noises
	Hoses			Other: _____

Notes: _____
_____
_____
_____
_____
_____

Operator's Name

_____

Operator's Signature

_____

Supervisor's Name

_____

Supervisor's Signature

_____

PROPANE FORKLIFT INSPECTION CHECKLIST

Date: _____ Shift: _____

Forklift Serial Number: _____

Hour Meter Start: _____ End: _____ Total Hours: _____

	Gas gauge			Hour Meter
	LPG tank and locator pin			Hydraulic Controls
	LPG tank hose			Lights - Head and Tail
	Accelerator			Lights - Warning
	Alarms			Mast
	Battery Connector			Oil Leaks
	Belt			Oil Pressure
	Brakes - Parking			Overhead Guard
	Engine Oil Level			Radiator Level
	Forks			Safety Equipment
	Fuel			Steering
	Gauges			Tires
	Horn			Unusual Noises
	Hoses			Other: _____

Notes: _____

_____

_____

_____

_____

_____

Operator's Name

_____

Operator's Signature

_____

Supervisor's Name

_____

Supervisor's Signature

_____

PROPANE FORKLIFT INSPECTION CHECKLIST

Date: _____ Shift: _____

Forklift Serial Number: _____

Hour Meter Start: _____ End: _____ Total Hours: _____

	Gas gauge		Hour Meter
	LPG tank and locator pin		Hydraulic Controls
	LPG tank hose		Lights - Head and Tail
	Accelerator		Lights - Warning
	Alarms		Mast
	Battery Connector		Oil Leaks
	Belt		Oil Pressure
	Brakes - Parking		Overhead Guard
	Engine Oil Level		Radiator Level
	Forks		Safety Equipment
	Fuel		Steering
	Gauges		Tires
	Horn		Unusual Noises
	Hoses		Other: _____

Notes: _____
_____
_____
_____
_____
_____

Operator's Name	Supervisor's Name
_____	_____
Operator's Signature	Supervisor's Signature
_____	_____

PROPANE FORKLIFT INSPECTION CHECKLIST

Date: _____ Shift: _____

Forklift Serial Number: _____

Hour Meter Start: _____ End: _____ Total Hours: _____

	Gas gauge		Hour Meter
	LPG tank and locator pin		Hydraulic Controls
	LPG tank hose		Lights - Head and Tail
	Accelerator		Lights - Warning
	Alarms		Mast
	Battery Connector		Oil Leaks
	Belt		Oil Pressure
	Brakes - Parking		Overhead Guard
	Engine Oil Level		Radiator Level
	Forks		Safety Equipment
	Fuel		Steering
	Gauges		Tires
	Horn		Unusual Noises
	Hoses		Other: _____

Notes: _____
_____
_____
_____
_____
_____

Operator's Name	Supervisor's Name
_____	_____
Operator's Signature	Supervisor's Signature
_____	_____

PROPANE FORKLIFT INSPECTION CHECKLIST

Date: _____ Shift: _____

Forklift Serial Number: _____

Hour Meter Start: _____ End: _____ Total Hours: _____

	Gas gauge		Hour Meter
	LPG tank and locator pin		Hydraulic Controls
	LPG tank hose		Lights - Head and Tail
	Accelerator		Lights - Warning
	Alarms		Mast
	Battery Connector		Oil Leaks
	Belt		Oil Pressure
	Brakes - Parking		Overhead Guard
	Engine Oil Level		Radiator Level
	Forks		Safety Equipment
	Fuel		Steering
	Gauges		Tires
	Horn		Unusual Noises
	Hoses		Other: _____

Notes: _____
_____
_____
_____
_____
_____

Operator's Name	Supervisor's Name
_____	_____
Operator's Signature	Supervisor's Signature
_____	_____

PROPANE FORKLIFT INSPECTION CHECKLIST

Date: _____ Shift: _____

Forklift Serial Number: _____

Hour Meter Start: _____ End: _____ Total Hours: _____

	Gas gauge		Hour Meter
	LPG tank and locator pin		Hydraulic Controls
	LPG tank hose		Lights - Head and Tail
	Accelerator		Lights - Warning
	Alarms		Mast
	Battery Connector		Oil Leaks
	Belt		Oil Pressure
	Brakes - Parking		Overhead Guard
	Engine Oil Level		Radiator Level
	Forks		Safety Equipment
	Fuel		Steering
	Gauges		Tires
	Horn		Unusual Noises
	Hoses		Other: _____

Notes: _____
_____
_____
_____
_____
_____

Operator's Name

_____

Operator's Signature

_____

Supervisor's Name

_____

Supervisor's Signature

_____

PROPANE FORKLIFT INSPECTION CHECKLIST

Date: _____ Shift: _____

Forklift Serial Number: _____

Hour Meter Start: _____ End: _____ Total Hours: _____

	Gas gauge		Hour Meter
	LPG tank and locator pin		Hydraulic Controls
	LPG tank hose		Lights - Head and Tail
	Accelerator		Lights - Warning
	Alarms		Mast
	Battery Connector		Oil Leaks
	Belt		Oil Pressure
	Brakes - Parking		Overhead Guard
	Engine Oil Level		Radiator Level
	Forks		Safety Equipment
	Fuel		Steering
	Gauges		Tires
	Horn		Unusual Noises
	Hoses		Other: _____

Notes: _____
_____
_____
_____
_____
_____
_____

Operator's Name	Supervisor's Name
_____	_____
Operator's Signature	Supervisor's Signature
_____	_____

PROPANE FORKLIFT INSPECTION CHECKLIST

Date: _____ Shift: _____

Forklift Serial Number: _____

Hour Meter Start: _____ End: _____ Total Hours: _____

	Gas gauge		Hour Meter
	LPG tank and locator pin		Hydraulic Controls
	LPG tank hose		Lights - Head and Tail
	Accelerator		Lights - Warning
	Alarms		Mast
	Battery Connector		Oil Leaks
	Belt		Oil Pressure
	Brakes - Parking		Overhead Guard
	Engine Oil Level		Radiator Level
	Forks		Safety Equipment
	Fuel		Steering
	Gauges		Tires
	Horn		Unusual Noises
	Hoses		Other: _____

Notes: _____
_____
_____
_____
_____
_____

Operator's Name

_____

Operator's Signature

_____

Supervisor's Name

_____

Supervisor's Signature

_____

PROPANE FORKLIFT INSPECTION CHECKLIST

Date: _____ Shift: _____

Forklift Serial Number: _____

Hour Meter Start: _____ End: _____ Total Hours: _____

	Gas gauge		Hour Meter
	LPG tank and locator pin		Hydraulic Controls
	LPG tank hose		Lights - Head and Tail
	Accelerator		Lights - Warning
	Alarms		Mast
	Battery Connector		Oil Leaks
	Belt		Oil Pressure
	Brakes - Parking		Overhead Guard
	Engine Oil Level		Radiator Level
	Forks		Safety Equipment
	Fuel		Steering
	Gauges		Tires
	Horn		Unusual Noises
	Hoses		Other: _____

Notes: _____
_____
_____
_____
_____
_____

Operator's Name
_____

Operator's Signature
_____

Supervisor's Name
_____

Supervisor's Signature
_____

PROPANE FORKLIFT INSPECTION CHECKLIST

Date: _____ Shift: _____

Forklift Serial Number: _____

Hour Meter Start: _____ End: _____ Total Hours: _____

	Gas gauge		Hour Meter
	LPG tank and locator pin		Hydraulic Controls
	LPG tank hose		Lights - Head and Tail
	Accelerator		Lights - Warning
	Alarms		Mast
	Battery Connector		Oil Leaks
	Belt		Oil Pressure
	Brakes - Parking		Overhead Guard
	Engine Oil Level		Radiator Level
	Forks		Safety Equipment
	Fuel		Steering
	Gauges		Tires
	Horn		Unusual Noises
	Hoses		Other: _____

Notes: _____
_____
_____
_____
_____
_____

Operator's Name	Supervisor's Name
_____	_____
Operator's Signature	Supervisor's Signature
_____	_____

PROPANE FORKLIFT INSPECTION CHECKLIST

Date: _____ Shift: _____

Forklift Serial Number: _____

Hour Meter Start: _____ End: _____ Total Hours: _____

	Gas gauge		Hour Meter
	LPG tank and locator pin		Hydraulic Controls
	LPG tank hose		Lights - Head and Tail
	Accelerator		Lights - Warning
	Alarms		Mast
	Battery Connector		Oil Leaks
	Belt		Oil Pressure
	Brakes - Parking		Overhead Guard
	Engine Oil Level		Radiator Level
	Forks		Safety Equipment
	Fuel		Steering
	Gauges		Tires
	Horn		Unusual Noises
	Hoses		Other: _____

Notes: _____
_____
_____
_____
_____
_____

Operator's Name

_____

Operator's Signature

_____

Supervisor's Name

_____

Supervisor's Signature

_____

PROPANE FORKLIFT INSPECTION CHECKLIST

Date: _____ Shift: _____

Forklift Serial Number: _____

Hour Meter Start: _____ End: _____ Total Hours: _____

	Gas gauge		Hour Meter
	LPG tank and locator pin		Hydraulic Controls
	LPG tank hose		Lights - Head and Tail
	Accelerator		Lights - Warning
	Alarms		Mast
	Battery Connector		Oil Leaks
	Belt		Oil Pressure
	Brakes - Parking		Overhead Guard
	Engine Oil Level		Radiator Level
	Forks		Safety Equipment
	Fuel		Steering
	Gauges		Tires
	Horn		Unusual Noises
	Hoses		Other: _____

Notes: _____
_____
_____
_____
_____
_____
_____

Operator's Name	Supervisor's Name
_____	_____
Operator's Signature	Supervisor's Signature
_____	_____

PROPANE FORKLIFT INSPECTION CHECKLIST

Date: _____ Shift: _____

Forklift Serial Number: _____

Hour Meter Start: _____ End: _____ Total Hours: _____

	Gas gauge			Hour Meter
	LPG tank and locator pin			Hydraulic Controls
	LPG tank hose			Lights - Head and Tail
	Accelerator			Lights - Warning
	Alarms			Mast
	Battery Connector			Oil Leaks
	Belt			Oil Pressure
	Brakes - Parking			Overhead Guard
	Engine Oil Level			Radiator Level
	Forks			Safety Equipment
	Fuel			Steering
	Gauges			Tires
	Horn			Unusual Noises
	Hoses			Other: _____

Notes: _____
_____
_____
_____
_____
_____
_____

Operator's Name
_____

Operator's Signature
_____

Supervisor's Name
_____

Supervisor's Signature
_____

PROPANE FORKLIFT INSPECTION CHECKLIST

Date: _____ Shift: _____

Forklift Serial Number: _____

Hour Meter Start: _____ End: _____ Total Hours: _____

	Gas gauge		Hour Meter
	LPG tank and locator pin		Hydraulic Controls
	LPG tank hose		Lights - Head and Tail
	Accelerator		Lights - Warning
	Alarms		Mast
	Battery Connector		Oil Leaks
	Belt		Oil Pressure
	Brakes - Parking		Overhead Guard
	Engine Oil Level		Radiator Level
	Forks		Safety Equipment
	Fuel		Steering
	Gauges		Tires
	Horn		Unusual Noises
	Hoses		Other: _____

Notes: _____
_____
_____
_____
_____
_____

Operator's Name

_____

Operator's Signature

_____

Supervisor's Name

_____

Supervisor's Signature

_____

PROPANE FORKLIFT INSPECTION CHECKLIST

Date: _____ Shift: _____

Forklift Serial Number: _____

Hour Meter Start: _____ End: _____ Total Hours: _____

	Gas gauge		Hour Meter	
	LPG tank and locator pin		Hydraulic Controls	
	LPG tank hose		Lights - Head and Tail	
	Accelerator		Lights - Warning	
	Alarms		Mast	
	Battery Connector		Oil Leaks	
	Belt		Oil Pressure	
	Brakes - Parking		Overhead Guard	
	Engine Oil Level		Radiator Level	
	Forks		Safety Equipment	
	Fuel		Steering	
	Gauges		Tires	
	Horn		Unusual Noises	
	Hoses		Other: _____	

Notes: _____
_____
_____
_____
_____
_____

Operator's Name

_____

Operator's Signature

_____

Supervisor's Name

_____

Supervisor's Signature

_____

PROPANE FORKLIFT INSPECTION CHECKLIST

Date: _____ Shift: _____

Forklift Serial Number: _____

Hour Meter Start: _____ End: _____ Total Hours: _____

	Gas gauge		Hour Meter
	LPG tank and locator pin		Hydraulic Controls
	LPG tank hose		Lights - Head and Tail
	Accelerator		Lights - Warning
	Alarms		Mast
	Battery Connector		Oil Leaks
	Belt		Oil Pressure
	Brakes - Parking		Overhead Guard
	Engine Oil Level		Radiator Level
	Forks		Safety Equipment
	Fuel		Steering
	Gauges		Tires
	Horn		Unusual Noises
	Hoses		Other: _____

Notes: _____
_____
_____
_____
_____
_____

Operator's Name

_____

Operator's Signature

_____

Supervisor's Name

_____

Supervisor's Signature

_____

PROPANE FORKLIFT INSPECTION CHECKLIST

Date: _____ Shift: _____

Forklift Serial Number: _____

Hour Meter Start: _____ End: _____ Total Hours: _____

	Gas gauge		Hour Meter
	LPG tank and locator pin		Hydraulic Controls
	LPG tank hose		Lights - Head and Tail
	Accelerator		Lights - Warning
	Alarms		Mast
	Battery Connector		Oil Leaks
	Belt		Oil Pressure
	Brakes - Parking		Overhead Guard
	Engine Oil Level		Radiator Level
	Forks		Safety Equipment
	Fuel		Steering
	Gauges		Tires
	Horn		Unusual Noises
	Hoses		Other: _____

Notes: _____
_____
_____
_____
_____
_____

Operator's Name	Supervisor's Name
_____	_____
Operator's Signature	Supervisor's Signature
_____	_____

PROPANE FORKLIFT INSPECTION CHECKLIST

Date: _____ Shift: _____

Forklift Serial Number: _____

Hour Meter Start: _____ End: _____ Total Hours: _____

	Gas gauge		Hour Meter
	LPG tank and locator pin		Hydraulic Controls
	LPG tank hose		Lights - Head and Tail
	Accelerator		Lights - Warning
	Alarms		Mast
	Battery Connector		Oil Leaks
	Belt		Oil Pressure
	Brakes - Parking		Overhead Guard
	Engine Oil Level		Radiator Level
	Forks		Safety Equipment
	Fuel		Steering
	Gauges		Tires
	Horn		Unusual Noises
	Hoses		Other: _____

Notes: _____

_____

_____

_____

_____

_____

Operator's Name

_____

Operator's Signature

_____

Supervisor's Name

_____

Supervisor's Signature

_____

PROPANE FORKLIFT INSPECTION CHECKLIST

Date: _____ Shift: _____

Forklift Serial Number: _____

Hour Meter Start: _____ End: _____ Total Hours: _____

	Gas gauge		Hour Meter
	LPG tank and locator pin		Hydraulic Controls
	LPG tank hose		Lights - Head and Tail
	Accelerator		Lights - Warning
	Alarms		Mast
	Battery Connector		Oil Leaks
	Belt		Oil Pressure
	Brakes - Parking		Overhead Guard
	Engine Oil Level		Radiator Level
	Forks		Safety Equipment
	Fuel		Steering
	Gauges		Tires
	Horn		Unusual Noises
	Hoses		Other: _____

Notes: _____
_____
_____
_____
_____
_____

Operator's Name

_____

Operator's Signature

_____

Supervisor's Name

_____

Supervisor's Signature

_____

PROPANE FORKLIFT INSPECTION CHECKLIST

Date: _____ Shift: _____

Forklift Serial Number: _____

Hour Meter Start: _____ End: _____ Total Hours: _____

	Gas gauge		Hour Meter
	LPG tank and locator pin		Hydraulic Controls
	LPG tank hose		Lights - Head and Tail
	Accelerator		Lights - Warning
	Alarms		Mast
	Battery Connector		Oil Leaks
	Belt		Oil Pressure
	Brakes - Parking		Overhead Guard
	Engine Oil Level		Radiator Level
	Forks		Safety Equipment
	Fuel		Steering
	Gauges		Tires
	Horn		Unusual Noises
	Hoses		Other: _____

Notes: _____

_____

_____

_____

_____

_____

Operator's Name

_____

Operator's Signature

_____

Supervisor's Name

_____

Supervisor's Signature

_____

PROPANE FORKLIFT INSPECTION CHECKLIST

Date: _____ Shift: _____

Forklift Serial Number: _____

Hour Meter Start: _____ End: _____ Total Hours: _____

	Gas gauge		Hour Meter
	LPG tank and locator pin		Hydraulic Controls
	LPG tank hose		Lights - Head and Tail
	Accelerator		Lights - Warning
	Alarms		Mast
	Battery Connector		Oil Leaks
	Belt		Oil Pressure
	Brakes - Parking		Overhead Guard
	Engine Oil Level		Radiator Level
	Forks		Safety Equipment
	Fuel		Steering
	Gauges		Tires
	Horn		Unusual Noises
	Hoses		Other: _____

Notes: _____
_____
_____
_____
_____
_____

Operator's Name

_____

Operator's Signature

_____

Supervisor's Name

_____

Supervisor's Signature

_____

PROPANE FORKLIFT INSPECTION CHECKLIST

Date: _____ Shift: _____

Forklift Serial Number: _____

Hour Meter Start: _____ End: _____ Total Hours: _____

	Gas gauge		Hour Meter
	LPG tank and locator pin		Hydraulic Controls
	LPG tank hose		Lights - Head and Tail
	Accelerator		Lights - Warning
	Alarms		Mast
	Battery Connector		Oil Leaks
	Belt		Oil Pressure
	Brakes - Parking		Overhead Guard
	Engine Oil Level		Radiator Level
	Forks		Safety Equipment
	Fuel		Steering
	Gauges		Tires
	Horn		Unusual Noises
	Hoses		Other: _____

Notes: _____
_____
_____
_____
_____
_____

Operator's Name	Supervisor's Name
Operator's Signature	Supervisor's Signature

PROPANE FORKLIFT INSPECTION CHECK

Date: _____ Shift: _____

Forklift Serial Number: _____

Hour Meter Start: _____ End: _____ Total Hours: _____

	Gas gauge		Hour Meter
	LPG tank and locator pin		Hydraulic Controls
	LPG tank hose		Lights - Head and Tail
	Accelerator		Lights - Warning
	Alarms		Mast
	Battery Connector		Oil Leaks
	Belt		Oil Pressure
	Brakes - Parking		Overhead Guard
	Engine Oil Level		Radiator Level
	Forks		Safety Equipment
	Fuel		Steering
	Gauges		Tires
	Horn		Unusual Noises
	Hoses		Other: _____

Notes: _____
_____
_____
_____
_____
_____

Operator's Name
_____

Operator's Signature
_____

Supervisor's Name
_____

Supervisor's Signature
_____

ROPANE FORKLIFT INSPECTION CHECKLIST

Date: _____ Shift: _____

Forklift Serial Number: _____

Hour Meter Start: _____ End: _____ Total Hours: _____

	Gas gauge		Hour Meter
	LPG tank and locator pin		Hydraulic Controls
	LPG tank hose		Lights - Head and Tail
	Accelerator		Lights - Warning
	Alarms		Mast
	Battery Connector		Oil Leaks
	Belt		Oil Pressure
	Brakes - Parking		Overhead Guard
	Engine Oil Level		Radiator Level
	Forks		Safety Equipment
	Fuel		Steering
	Gauges		Tires
	Horn		Unusual Noises
	Hoses		Other: _____

Notes: _____
_____
_____
_____
_____
_____

Operator's Name

_____

Operator's Signature

_____

Supervisor's Name

_____

Supervisor's Signature

_____

PROPANE FORKLIFT INSPECTION CHECKLIST

Date: _____ Shift: _____

Forklift Serial Number: _____

Hour Meter Start: _____ End: _____ Total Hours: _____

	Gas gauge		Hour Meter
	LPG tank and locator pin		Hydraulic Controls
	LPG tank hose		Lights - Head and Tail
	Accelerator		Lights - Warning
	Alarms		Mast
	Battery Connector		Oil Leaks
	Belt		Oil Pressure
	Brakes - Parking		Overhead Guard
	Engine Oil Level		Radiator Level
	Forks		Safety Equipment
	Fuel		Steering
	Gauges		Tires
	Horn		Unusual Noises
	Hoses		Other: _____

Notes: _____
_____
_____
_____
_____
_____
_____

Operator's Name	Supervisor's Name
_____	_____
Operator's Signature	Supervisor's Signature
_____	_____

PROPANE FORKLIFT INSPECTION CHECKLIST

Date: _____ Shift: _____

Forklift Serial Number: _____

Hour Meter Start: _____ End: _____ Total Hours: _____

	Gas gauge		Hour Meter
	LPG tank and locator pin		Hydraulic Controls
	LPG tank hose		Lights - Head and Tail
	Accelerator		Lights - Warning
	Alarms		Mast
	Battery Connector		Oil Leaks
	Belt		Oil Pressure
	Brakes - Parking		Overhead Guard
	Engine Oil Level		Radiator Level
	Forks		Safety Equipment
	Fuel		Steering
	Gauges		Tires
	Horn		Unusual Noises
	Hoses		Other: _____

Notes: _____

_____

_____

_____

_____

_____

Operator's Name

_____

Operator's Signature

_____

Supervisor's Name

_____

Supervisor's Signature

_____

PROPANE FORKLIFT INSPECTION CHECKLIST

Date: _____ Shift: _____

Forklift Serial Number: _____

Hour Meter Start: _____ End: _____ Total Hours: _____

	Gas gauge		Hour Meter
	LPG tank and locator pin		Hydraulic Controls
	LPG tank hose		Lights - Head and Tail
	Accelerator		Lights - Warning
	Alarms		Mast
	Battery Connector		Oil Leaks
	Belt		Oil Pressure
	Brakes - Parking		Overhead Guard
	Engine Oil Level		Radiator Level
	Forks		Safety Equipment
	Fuel		Steering
	Gauges		Tires
	Horn		Unusual Noises
	Hoses		Other: _____

Notes: _____
_____
_____
_____
_____
_____

Operator's Name	Supervisor's Name
_____	_____
Operator's Signature	Supervisor's Signature
_____	_____

PROPANE FORKLIFT INSPECTION CHECKLIST

Date: _____ Shift: _____

Forklift Serial Number: _____

Hour Meter Start: _____ End: _____ Total Hours: _____

	Gas gauge		Hour Meter
	LPG tank and locator pin		Hydraulic Controls
	LPG tank hose		Lights - Head and Tail
	Accelerator		Lights - Warning
	Alarms		Mast
	Battery Connector		Oil Leaks
	Belt		Oil Pressure
	Brakes - Parking		Overhead Guard
	Engine Oil Level		Radiator Level
	Forks		Safety Equipment
	Fuel		Steering
	Gauges		Tires
	Horn		Unusual Noises
	Hoses		Other: _____

Notes: _____
_____
_____
_____
_____
_____

Operator's Name	Supervisor's Name
_____	_____
Operator's Signature	Supervisor's Signature
_____	_____

PROPANE FORKLIFT INSPECTION CHECKLIST

Date: _____ Shift: _____

Forklift Serial Number: _____

Hour Meter Start: _____ End: _____ Total Hours: _____

	Gas gauge		Hour Meter
	LPG tank and locator pin		Hydraulic Controls
	LPG tank hose		Lights - Head and Tail
	Accelerator		Lights - Warning
	Alarms		Mast
	Battery Connector		Oil Leaks
	Belt		Oil Pressure
	Brakes - Parking		Overhead Guard
	Engine Oil Level		Radiator Level
	Forks		Safety Equipment
	Fuel		Steering
	Gauges		Tires
	Horn		Unusual Noises
	Hoses		Other: _____

Notes: _____

_____

_____

_____

_____

_____

_____

Operator's Name

_____

Operator's Signature

_____

Supervisor's Name

_____

Supervisor's Signature

_____

PROPANE FORKLIFT INSPECTION CHECKLIST

Date: _____ Shift: _____

Forklift Serial Number: _____

Hour Meter Start: _____ End: _____ Total Hours: _____

	Gas gauge		Hour Meter
	LPG tank and locator pin		Hydraulic Controls
	LPG tank hose		Lights - Head and Tail
	Accelerator		Lights - Warning
	Alarms		Mast
	Battery Connector		Oil Leaks
	Belt		Oil Pressure
	Brakes - Parking		Overhead Guard
	Engine Oil Level		Radiator Level
	Forks		Safety Equipment
	Fuel		Steering
	Gauges		Tires
	Horn		Unusual Noises
	Hoses		Other: _____

Notes: _____
_____
_____
_____
_____
_____

Operator's Name

_____

Operator's Signature

_____

Supervisor's Name

_____

Supervisor's Signature

_____

PROPANE FORKLIFT INSPECTION CHECKLIST

Date: _____ Shift: _____

Forklift Serial Number: _____

Hour Meter Start: _____ End: _____ Total Hours: _____

	Gas gauge		Hour Meter
	LPG tank and locator pin		Hydraulic Controls
	LPG tank hose		Lights - Head and Tail
	Accelerator		Lights - Warning
	Alarms		Mast
	Battery Connector		Oil Leaks
	Belt		Oil Pressure
	Brakes - Parking		Overhead Guard
	Engine Oil Level		Radiator Level
	Forks		Safety Equipment
	Fuel		Steering
	Gauges		Tires
	Horn		Unusual Noises
	Hoses		Other: _____

Notes: _____
_____
_____
_____
_____
_____

Operator's Name

_____

Operator's Signature

_____

Supervisor's Name

_____

Supervisor's Signature

_____

PROPANE FORKLIFT INSPECTION CHECKLIST

Date: _____ Shift: _____

Forklift Serial Number: _____

Hour Meter Start: _____ End: _____ Total Hours: _____

	Gas gauge		Hour Meter
	LPG tank and locator pin		Hydraulic Controls
	LPG tank hose		Lights - Head and Tail
	Accelerator		Lights - Warning
	Alarms		Mast
	Battery Connector		Oil Leaks
	Belt		Oil Pressure
	Brakes - Parking		Overhead Guard
	Engine Oil Level		Radiator Level
	Forks		Safety Equipment
	Fuel		Steering
	Gauges		Tires
	Horn		Unusual Noises
	Hoses		Other: _____

Notes: _____

_____

_____

_____

_____

_____

Operator's Name

_____

Operator's Signature

_____

Supervisor's Name

_____

Supervisor's Signature

_____

PROPANE FORKLIFT INSPECTION CHECKLIST

Date: _____ Shift: _____

Forklift Serial Number: _____

Hour Meter Start: _____ End: _____ Total Hours: _____

	Gas gauge		Hour Meter
	LPG tank and locator pin		Hydraulic Controls
	LPG tank hose		Lights - Head and Tail
	Accelerator		Lights - Warning
	Alarms		Mast
	Battery Connector		Oil Leaks
	Belt		Oil Pressure
	Brakes - Parking		Overhead Guard
	Engine Oil Level		Radiator Level
	Forks		Safety Equipment
	Fuel		Steering
	Gauges		Tires
	Horn		Unusual Noises
	Hoses		Other: _____

Notes: _____
_____
_____
_____
_____
_____

Operator's Name

_____

Operator's Signature

_____

Supervisor's Name

_____

Supervisor's Signature

_____

PROPANE FORKLIFT INSPECTION CHECKLIST

Date: _____ Shift: _____

Forklift Serial Number: _____

Hour Meter Start: _____ End: _____ Total Hours: _____

	Gas gauge		Hour Meter
	LPG tank and locator pin		Hydraulic Controls
	LPG tank hose		Lights - Head and Tail
	Accelerator		Lights - Warning
	Alarms		Mast
	Battery Connector		Oil Leaks
	Belt		Oil Pressure
	Brakes - Parking		Overhead Guard
	Engine Oil Level		Radiator Level
	Forks		Safety Equipment
	Fuel		Steering
	Gauges		Tires
	Horn		Unusual Noises
	Hoses		Other: _____

Notes: _____
_____
_____
_____
_____
_____

Operator's Name

_____

Operator's Signature

_____

Supervisor's Name

_____

Supervisor's Signature

_____

PROPANE FORKLIFT INSPECTION CHECKLIST

Date: _____ Shift: _____

Forklift Serial Number: _____

Hour Meter Start: _____ End: _____ Total Hours: _____

	Gas gauge		Hour Meter
	LPG tank and locator pin		Hydraulic Controls
	LPG tank hose		Lights - Head and Tail
	Accelerator		Lights - Warning
	Alarms		Mast
	Battery Connector		Oil Leaks
	Belt		Oil Pressure
	Brakes - Parking		Overhead Guard
	Engine Oil Level		Radiator Level
	Forks		Safety Equipment
	Fuel		Steering
	Gauges		Tires
	Horn		Unusual Noises
	Hoses		Other: _____

Notes: _____
_____
_____
_____
_____
_____

Operator's Name	Supervisor's Name
_____	_____
Operator's Signature	Supervisor's Signature
_____	_____

PROPANE FORKLIFT INSPECTION CHECKLIST

Date: _____ Shift: _____

Forklift Serial Number: _____

Hour Meter Start: _____ End: _____ Total Hours: _____

	Gas gauge		Hour Meter
	LPG tank and locator pin		Hydraulic Controls
	LPG tank hose		Lights - Head and Tail
	Accelerator		Lights - Warning
	Alarms		Mast
	Battery Connector		Oil Leaks
	Belt		Oil Pressure
	Brakes - Parking		Overhead Guard
	Engine Oil Level		Radiator Level
	Forks		Safety Equipment
	Fuel		Steering
	Gauges		Tires
	Horn		Unusual Noises
	Hoses		Other: _____

Notes: _____
_____
_____
_____
_____
_____

Operator's Name
_____

Operator's Signature
_____

Supervisor's Name
_____

Supervisor's Signature
_____

PROPANE FORKLIFT INSPECTION CHECKLIST

Date: _____ Shift: _____

Forklift Serial Number: _____

Hour Meter Start: _____ End: _____ Total Hours: _____

	Gas gauge		Hour Meter
	LPG tank and locator pin		Hydraulic Controls
	LPG tank hose		Lights - Head and Tail
	Accelerator		Lights - Warning
	Alarms		Mast
	Battery Connector		Oil Leaks
	Belt		Oil Pressure
	Brakes - Parking		Overhead Guard
	Engine Oil Level		Radiator Level
	Forks		Safety Equipment
	Fuel		Steering
	Gauges		Tires
	Horn		Unusual Noises
	Hoses		Other: _____

Notes: _____
_____
_____
_____
_____
_____

Operator's Name	Supervisor's Name
_____	_____
Operator's Signature	Supervisor's Signature
_____	_____

PROPANE FORKLIFT INSPECTION CHECKLIST

Date: _____ Shift: _____

Forklift Serial Number: _____

Hour Meter Start: _____ End: _____ Total Hours: _____

	Gas gauge		Hour Meter
	LPG tank and locator pin		Hydraulic Controls
	LPG tank hose		Lights - Head and Tail
	Accelerator		Lights - Warning
	Alarms		Mast
	Battery Connector		Oil Leaks
	Belt		Oil Pressure
	Brakes - Parking		Overhead Guard
	Engine Oil Level		Radiator Level
	Forks		Safety Equipment
	Fuel		Steering
	Gauges		Tires
	Horn		Unusual Noises
	Hoses		Other: _____

Notes: _____

_____

_____

_____

_____

_____

Operator's Name

_____

Operator's Signature

_____

Supervisor's Name

_____

Supervisor's Signature

_____

PROPANE FORKLIFT INSPECTION CHECKLIST

Date: _____ Shift: _____

Forklift Serial Number: _____

Hour Meter Start: _____ End: _____ Total Hours: _____

	Gas gauge		Hour Meter
	LPG tank and locator pin		Hydraulic Controls
	LPG tank hose		Lights - Head and Tail
	Accelerator		Lights - Warning
	Alarms		Mast
	Battery Connector		Oil Leaks
	Belt		Oil Pressure
	Brakes - Parking		Overhead Guard
	Engine Oil Level		Radiator Level
	Forks		Safety Equipment
	Fuel		Steering
	Gauges		Tires
	Horn		Unusual Noises
	Hoses		Other: _____

Notes: _____
_____
_____
_____
_____
_____
_____

Operator's Name

_____

Operator's Signature

_____

Supervisor's Name

_____

Supervisor's Signature

_____

PROPANE FORKLIFT INSPECTION CHECKLIST

Date: _____ Shift: _____

Forklift Serial Number: _____

Hour Meter Start: _____ End: _____ Total Hours: _____

	Gas gauge		Hour Meter
	LPG tank and locator pin		Hydraulic Controls
	LPG tank hose		Lights - Head and Tail
	Accelerator		Lights - Warning
	Alarms		Mast
	Battery Connector		Oil Leaks
	Belt		Oil Pressure
	Brakes - Parking		Overhead Guard
	Engine Oil Level		Radiator Level
	Forks		Safety Equipment
	Fuel		Steering
	Gauges		Tires
	Horn		Unusual Noises
	Hoses		Other: _____

Notes: _____
_____
_____
_____
_____
_____

Operator's Name	Supervisor's Name
_____	_____
Operator's Signature	Supervisor's Signature
_____	_____

PROPANE FORKLIFT INSPECTION CHECKLIST

Date: _____ Shift: _____

Forklift Serial Number: _____

Hour Meter Start: _____ End: _____ Total Hours: _____

	Gas gauge		Hour Meter
	LPG tank and locator pin		Hydraulic Controls
	LPG tank hose		Lights - Head and Tail
	Accelerator		Lights - Warning
	Alarms		Mast
	Battery Connector		Oil Leaks
	Belt		Oil Pressure
	Brakes - Parking		Overhead Guard
	Engine Oil Level		Radiator Level
	Forks		Safety Equipment
	Fuel		Steering
	Gauges		Tires
	Horn		Unusual Noises
	Hoses		Other: _____

Notes: _____
_____
_____
_____
_____
_____
_____

Operator's Name

_____
Operator's Signature

_____

Supervisor's Name

_____
Supervisor's Signature

_____

PROPANE FORKLIFT INSPECTION CHECKLIST

Date: _____ Shift: _____

Forklift Serial Number: _____

Hour Meter Start: _____ End: _____ Total Hours: _____

	Gas gauge			Hour Meter
	LPG tank and locator pin			Hydraulic Controls
	LPG tank hose			Lights - Head and Tail
	Accelerator			Lights - Warning
	Alarms			Mast
	Battery Connector			Oil Leaks
	Belt			Oil Pressure
	Brakes - Parking			Overhead Guard
	Engine Oil Level			Radiator Level
	Forks			Safety Equipment
	Fuel			Steering
	Gauges			Tires
	Horn			Unusual Noises
	Hoses			Other: _____

Notes: _____
_____
_____
_____
_____
_____
_____

Operator's Name

_____

Operator's Signature

_____

Supervisor's Name

_____

Supervisor's Signature

_____

PROPANE FORKLIFT INSPECTION CHECKLIST

Date: _____ Shift: _____

Forklift Serial Number: _____

Hour Meter Start: _____ End: _____ Total Hours: _____

	Gas gauge		Hour Meter
	LPG tank and locator pin		Hydraulic Controls
	LPG tank hose		Lights - Head and Tail
	Accelerator		Lights - Warning
	Alarms		Mast
	Battery Connector		Oil Leaks
	Belt		Oil Pressure
	Brakes - Parking		Overhead Guard
	Engine Oil Level		Radiator Level
	Forks		Safety Equipment
	Fuel		Steering
	Gauges		Tires
	Horn		Unusual Noises
	Hoses		Other: _____

Notes: _____
_____
_____
_____
_____
_____

Operator's Name

_____
Operator's Signature

_____

Supervisor's Name

_____
Supervisor's Signature

_____

PROPANE FORKLIFT INSPECTION CHECKLIST

Date: _____ Shift: _____

Forklift Serial Number: _____

Hour Meter Start: _____ End: _____ Total Hours: _____

	Gas gauge		Hour Meter
	LPG tank and locator pin		Hydraulic Controls
	LPG tank hose		Lights - Head and Tail
	Accelerator		Lights - Warning
	Alarms		Mast
	Battery Connector		Oil Leaks
	Belt		Oil Pressure
	Brakes - Parking		Overhead Guard
	Engine Oil Level		Radiator Level
	Forks		Safety Equipment
	Fuel		Steering
	Gauges		Tires
	Horn		Unusual Noises
	Hoses		Other: _____

Notes: _____
_____
_____
_____
_____
_____

Operator's Name	Supervisor's Name
_____	_____
Operator's Signature	Supervisor's Signature
_____	_____

PROPANE FORKLIFT INSPECTION CHECKLIST

Date: _____ Shift: _____

Forklift Serial Number: _____

Hour Meter Start: _____ End: _____ Total Hours: _____

	Gas gauge		Hour Meter
	LPG tank and locator pin		Hydraulic Controls
	LPG tank hose		Lights - Head and Tail
	Accelerator		Lights - Warning
	Alarms		Mast
	Battery Connector		Oil Leaks
	Belt		Oil Pressure
	Brakes - Parking		Overhead Guard
	Engine Oil Level		Radiator Level
	Forks		Safety Equipment
	Fuel		Steering
	Gauges		Tires
	Horn		Unusual Noises
	Hoses		Other: _____

Notes: _____
_____
_____
_____
_____
_____

Operator's Name	Supervisor's Name
_____	_____
Operator's Signature	Supervisor's Signature
_____	_____

PROPANE FORKLIFT INSPECTION CHECKLIST

Date: _____ Shift: _____

Forklift Serial Number: _____

Hour Meter Start: _____ End: _____ Total Hours: _____

	Gas gauge		Hour Meter
	LPG tank and locator pin		Hydraulic Controls
	LPG tank hose		Lights - Head and Tail
	Accelerator		Lights - Warning
	Alarms		Mast
	Battery Connector		Oil Leaks
	Belt		Oil Pressure
	Brakes - Parking		Overhead Guard
	Engine Oil Level		Radiator Level
	Forks		Safety Equipment
	Fuel		Steering
	Gauges		Tires
	Horn		Unusual Noises
	Hoses		Other: _____

Notes: _____
_____
_____
_____
_____
_____
_____

Operator's Name

_____

Operator's Signature

_____

Supervisor's Name

_____

Supervisor's Signature

_____

PROPANE FORKLIFT INSPECTION CHECKLIST

Date: _____ Shift: _____

Forklift Serial Number: _____

Hour Meter Start: _____ End: _____ Total Hours: _____

	Gas gauge		Hour Meter
	LPG tank and locator pin		Hydraulic Controls
	LPG tank hose		Lights - Head and Tail
	Accelerator		Lights - Warning
	Alarms		Mast
	Battery Connector		Oil Leaks
	Belt		Oil Pressure
	Brakes - Parking		Overhead Guard
	Engine Oil Level		Radiator Level
	Forks		Safety Equipment
	Fuel		Steering
	Gauges		Tires
	Horn		Unusual Noises
	Hoses		Other: _____

Notes: _____
_____
_____
_____
_____
_____

Operator's Name	Supervisor's Name
_____	_____
Operator's Signature	Supervisor's Signature
_____	_____

PROPANE FORKLIFT INSPECTION CHECKLIST

Date: _____ Shift: _____

Forklift Serial Number: _____

Hour Meter Start: _____ End: _____ Total Hours: _____

	Gas gauge			Hour Meter
	LPG tank and locator pin			Hydraulic Controls
	LPG tank hose			Lights - Head and Tail
	Accelerator			Lights - Warning
	Alarms			Mast
	Battery Connector			Oil Leaks
	Belt			Oil Pressure
	Brakes - Parking			Overhead Guard
	Engine Oil Level			Radiator Level
	Forks			Safety Equipment
	Fuel			Steering
	Gauges			Tires
	Horn			Unusual Noises
	Hoses			Other: _____

Notes: _____
_____
_____
_____
_____
_____

Operator's Name	Supervisor's Name
Operator's Signature	Supervisor's Signature

PROPANE FORKLIFT INSPECTION CHECKLIST

Date: _____ Shift: _____

Forklift Serial Number: _____

Hour Meter Start: _____ End: _____ Total Hours: _____

	Gas gauge		Hour Meter
	LPG tank and locator pin		Hydraulic Controls
	LPG tank hose		Lights - Head and Tail
	Accelerator		Lights - Warning
	Alarms		Mast
	Battery Connector		Oil Leaks
	Belt		Oil Pressure
	Brakes - Parking		Overhead Guard
	Engine Oil Level		Radiator Level
	Forks		Safety Equipment
	Fuel		Steering
	Gauges		Tires
	Horn		Unusual Noises
	Hoses		Other: _____

Notes: _____
_____
_____
_____
_____
_____

Operator's Name	Supervisor's Name
_____	_____
Operator's Signature	Supervisor's Signature
_____	_____

PROPANE FORKLIFT INSPECTION CHECKLIST

Date: _____ Shift: _____

Forklift Serial Number: _____

Hour Meter Start: _____ End: _____ Total Hours: _____

	Gas gauge		Hour Meter
	LPG tank and locator pin		Hydraulic Controls
	LPG tank hose		Lights - Head and Tail
	Accelerator		Lights - Warning
	Alarms		Mast
	Battery Connector		Oil Leaks
	Belt		Oil Pressure
	Brakes - Parking		Overhead Guard
	Engine Oil Level		Radiator Level
	Forks		Safety Equipment
	Fuel		Steering
	Gauges		Tires
	Horn		Unusual Noises
	Hoses		Other: _____

Notes: _____
_____
_____
_____
_____
_____

Operator's Name

_____

Operator's Signature

_____

Supervisor's Name

_____

Supervisor's Signature

_____

PROPANE FORKLIFT INSPECTION CHECKLIST

Date: _____ Shift: _____

Forklift Serial Number: _____

Hour Meter Start: _____ End: _____ Total Hours: _____

	Gas gauge		Hour Meter
	LPG tank and locator pin		Hydraulic Controls
	LPG tank hose		Lights - Head and Tail
	Accelerator		Lights - Warning
	Alarms		Mast
	Battery Connector		Oil Leaks
	Belt		Oil Pressure
	Brakes - Parking		Overhead Guard
	Engine Oil Level		Radiator Level
	Forks		Safety Equipment
	Fuel		Steering
	Gauges		Tires
	Horn		Unusual Noises
	Hoses		Other: _____

Notes: _____
_____
_____
_____
_____
_____
_____

Operator's Name	Supervisor's Name
_____	_____
Operator's Signature	Supervisor's Signature
_____	_____

PROPANE FORKLIFT INSPECTION CHECKLIST

Date: _____ Shift: _____

Forklift Serial Number: _____

Hour Meter Start: _____ End: _____ Total Hours: _____

Gas gauge		Hour Meter
LPG tank and locator pin		Hydraulic Controls
LPG tank hose		Lights - Head and Tail
Accelerator		Lights - Warning
Alarms		Mast
Battery Connector		Oil Leaks
Belt		Oil Pressure
Brakes - Parking		Overhead Guard
Engine Oil Level		Radiator Level
Forks		Safety Equipment
Fuel		Steering
Gauges		Tires
Horn		Unusual Noises
Hoses		Other: _____

Notes: _____
_____
_____
_____
_____
_____

Operator's Name	Supervisor's Name
_____	_____
Operator's Signature	Supervisor's Signature
_____	_____

PROPANE FORKLIFT INSPECTION CHECKLIST

Date: _____ Shift: _____

Forklift Serial Number: _____

Hour Meter Start: _____ End: _____ Total Hours: _____

	Gas gauge		Hour Meter
	LPG tank and locator pin		Hydraulic Controls
	LPG tank hose		Lights - Head and Tail
	Accelerator		Lights - Warning
	Alarms		Mast
	Battery Connector		Oil Leaks
	Belt		Oil Pressure
	Brakes - Parking		Overhead Guard
	Engine Oil Level		Radiator Level
	Forks		Safety Equipment
	Fuel		Steering
	Gauges		Tires
	Horn		Unusual Noises
	Hoses		Other: _____

Notes: _____
_____
_____
_____
_____
_____

Operator's Name

_____

Operator's Signature

_____

Supervisor's Name

_____

Supervisor's Signature

_____

PROPANE FORKLIFT INSPECTION CHECKLIST

Date: _____ Shift: _____

Forklift Serial Number: _____

Hour Meter Start: _____ End: _____ Total Hours: _____

	Gas gauge		Hour Meter
	LPG tank and locator pin		Hydraulic Controls
	LPG tank hose		Lights - Head and Tail
	Accelerator		Lights - Warning
	Alarms		Mast
	Battery Connector		Oil Leaks
	Belt		Oil Pressure
	Brakes - Parking		Overhead Guard
	Engine Oil Level		Radiator Level
	Forks		Safety Equipment
	Fuel		Steering
	Gauges		Tires
	Horn		Unusual Noises
	Hoses		Other: _____

Notes: _____
_____
_____
_____
_____
_____
_____

Operator's Name	Supervisor's Name
_____	_____
Operator's Signature	Supervisor's Signature
_____	_____

PROPANE FORKLIFT INSPECTION CHECKLIST

Date: _____ Shift: _____

Forklift Serial Number: _____

Hour Meter Start: _____ End: _____ Total Hours: _____

	Gas gauge		Hour Meter
	LPG tank and locator pin		Hydraulic Controls
	LPG tank hose		Lights - Head and Tail
	Accelerator		Lights - Warning
	Alarms		Mast
	Battery Connector		Oil Leaks
	Belt		Oil Pressure
	Brakes - Parking		Overhead Guard
	Engine Oil Level		Radiator Level
	Forks		Safety Equipment
	Fuel		Steering
	Gauges		Tires
	Horn		Unusual Noises
	Hoses		Other: _____

Notes: _____
_____
_____
_____
_____
_____
_____

Operator's Name

_____

Operator's Signature

_____

Supervisor's Name

_____

Supervisor's Signature

_____

PROPANE FORKLIFT INSPECTION CHECKLIST

Date: _____ Shift: _____

Forklift Serial Number: _____

Hour Meter Start: _____ End: _____ Total Hours: _____

	Gas gauge		Hour Meter
	LPG tank and locator pin		Hydraulic Controls
	LPG tank hose		Lights - Head and Tail
	Accelerator		Lights - Warning
	Alarms		Mast
	Battery Connector		Oil Leaks
	Belt		Oil Pressure
	Brakes - Parking		Overhead Guard
	Engine Oil Level		Radiator Level
	Forks		Safety Equipment
	Fuel		Steering
	Gauges		Tires
	Horn		Unusual Noises
	Hoses		Other: _____

Notes: _____
_____
_____
_____
_____
_____

Operator's Name	Supervisor's Name
_____	_____
Operator's Signature	Supervisor's Signature
_____	_____

PROPANE FORKLIFT INSPECTION CHECKLIST

Date: _____ Shift: _____

Forklift Serial Number: _____

Hour Meter Start: _____ End: _____ Total Hours: _____

	Gas gauge		Hour Meter
	LPG tank and locator pin		Hydraulic Controls
	LPG tank hose		Lights - Head and Tail
	Accelerator		Lights - Warning
	Alarms		Mast
	Battery Connector		Oil Leaks
	Belt		Oil Pressure
	Brakes - Parking		Overhead Guard
	Engine Oil Level		Radiator Level
	Forks		Safety Equipment
	Fuel		Steering
	Gauges		Tires
	Horn		Unusual Noises
	Hoses		Other: _____

Notes: _____
_____
_____
_____
_____
_____
_____

Operator's Name	Supervisor's Name
_____	_____
Operator's Signature	Supervisor's Signature
_____	_____

PROPANE FORKLIFT INSPECTION CHECKLIST

Date: _____ Shift: _____

Forklift Serial Number: _____

Hour Meter Start: _____ End: _____ Total Hours: _____

	Gas gauge		Hour Meter
	LPG tank and locator pin		Hydraulic Controls
	LPG tank hose		Lights - Head and Tail
	Accelerator		Lights - Warning
	Alarms		Mast
	Battery Connector		Oil Leaks
	Belt		Oil Pressure
	Brakes - Parking		Overhead Guard
	Engine Oil Level		Radiator Level
	Forks		Safety Equipment
	Fuel		Steering
	Gauges		Tires
	Horn		Unusual Noises
	Hoses		Other: _____

Notes: _____
_____
_____
_____
_____
_____
_____

Operator's Name

_____

Operator's Signature

_____

Supervisor's Name

_____

Supervisor's Signature

_____

PROPANE FORKLIFT INSPECTION CHECKLIST

Date: _____ Shift: _____

Forklift Serial Number: _____

Hour Meter Start: _____ End: _____ Total Hours: _____

	Gas gauge		Hour Meter
	LPG tank and locator pin		Hydraulic Controls
	LPG tank hose		Lights - Head and Tail
	Accelerator		Lights - Warning
	Alarms		Mast
	Battery Connector		Oil Leaks
	Belt		Oil Pressure
	Brakes - Parking		Overhead Guard
	Engine Oil Level		Radiator Level
	Forks		Safety Equipment
	Fuel		Steering
	Gauges		Tires
	Horn		Unusual Noises
	Hoses		Other: _____

Notes: _____
_____
_____
_____
_____
_____

Operator's Name
_____
Operator's Signature
_____

Supervisor's Name
_____
Supervisor's Signature
_____

PROPANE FORKLIFT INSPECTION CHECKLIST

Date: _____ Shift: _____

Forklift Serial Number: _____

Hour Meter Start: _____ End: _____ Total Hours: _____

	Gas gauge		Hour Meter
	LPG tank and locator pin		Hydraulic Controls
	LPG tank hose		Lights - Head and Tail
	Accelerator		Lights - Warning
	Alarms		Mast
	Battery Connector		Oil Leaks
	Belt		Oil Pressure
	Brakes - Parking		Overhead Guard
	Engine Oil Level		Radiator Level
	Forks		Safety Equipment
	Fuel		Steering
	Gauges		Tires
	Horn		Unusual Noises
	Hoses		Other: _____

Notes: _____
_____
_____
_____
_____
_____

Operator's Name	Supervisor's Name
_____	_____
Operator's Signature	Supervisor's Signature
_____	_____

PROPANE FORKLIFT INSPECTION CHECKLIST

Date: _____ Shift: _____

Forklift Serial Number: _____

Hour Meter Start: _____ End: _____ Total Hours: _____

	Gas gauge		Hour Meter
	LPG tank and locator pin		Hydraulic Controls
	LPG tank hose		Lights - Head and Tail
	Accelerator		Lights - Warning
	Alarms		Mast
	Battery Connector		Oil Leaks
	Belt		Oil Pressure
	Brakes - Parking		Overhead Guard
	Engine Oil Level		Radiator Level
	Forks		Safety Equipment
	Fuel		Steering
	Gauges		Tires
	Horn		Unusual Noises
	Hoses		Other: _____

Notes: _____
_____
_____
_____
_____
_____

Operator's Name	Supervisor's Name
_____	_____
Operator's Signature	Supervisor's Signature
_____	_____

PROPANE FORKLIFT INSPECTION CHECKLIST

Date: _____ Shift: _____

Forklift Serial Number: _____

Hour Meter Start: _____ End: _____ Total Hours: _____

	Gas gauge		Hour Meter
	LPG tank and locator pin		Hydraulic Controls
	LPG tank hose		Lights - Head and Tail
	Accelerator		Lights - Warning
	Alarms		Mast
	Battery Connector		Oil Leaks
	Belt		Oil Pressure
	Brakes - Parking		Overhead Guard
	Engine Oil Level		Radiator Level
	Forks		Safety Equipment
	Fuel		Steering
	Gauges		Tires
	Horn		Unusual Noises
	Hoses		Other: _____

Notes: _____

_____

_____

_____

_____

_____

Operator's Name

_____

Operator's Signature

_____

Supervisor's Name

_____

Supervisor's Signature

_____

PROPANE FORKLIFT INSPECTION CHECKLIST

Date: _____ Shift: _____

Forklift Serial Number: _____

Hour Meter Start: _____ End: _____ Total Hours: _____

	Gas gauge		Hour Meter
	LPG tank and locator pin		Hydraulic Controls
	LPG tank hose		Lights - Head and Tail
	Accelerator		Lights - Warning
	Alarms		Mast
	Battery Connector		Oil Leaks
	Belt		Oil Pressure
	Brakes - Parking		Overhead Guard
	Engine Oil Level		Radiator Level
	Forks		Safety Equipment
	Fuel		Steering
	Gauges		Tires
	Horn		Unusual Noises
	Hoses		Other: _____

Notes: _____

_____

_____

_____

_____

_____

_____

Operator's Name	Supervisor's Name
_____	_____
Operator's Signature	Supervisor's Signature
_____	_____

PROPANE FORKLIFT INSPECTION CHECKLIST

Date: _____ Shift: _____

Forklift Serial Number: _____

Hour Meter Start:_____ End:_____ Total Hours:_____

	Gas gauge		Hour Meter
	LPG tank and locator pin		Hydraulic Controls
	LPG tank hose		Lights - Head and Tail
	Accelerator		Lights - Warning
	Alarms		Mast
	Battery Connector		Oil Leaks
	Belt		Oil Pressure
	Brakes - Parking		Overhead Guard
	Engine Oil Level		Radiator Level
	Forks		Safety Equipment
	Fuel		Steering
	Gauges		Tires
	Horn		Unusual Noises
	Hoses		Other: _____

Notes: _____
_____
_____
_____
_____
_____

Operator's Name
_____

Operator's Signature
_____

Supervisor's Name
_____

Supervisor's Signature
_____

PROPANE FORKLIFT INSPECTION CHECKLIST

Date: _____ Shift: _____

Forklift Serial Number: _____

Hour Meter Start: _____ End: _____ Total Hours: _____

	Gas gauge		Hour Meter
	LPG tank and locator pin		Hydraulic Controls
	LPG tank hose		Lights - Head and Tail
	Accelerator		Lights - Warning
	Alarms		Mast
	Battery Connector		Oil Leaks
	Belt		Oil Pressure
	Brakes - Parking		Overhead Guard
	Engine Oil Level		Radiator Level
	Forks		Safety Equipment
	Fuel		Steering
	Gauges		Tires
	Horn		Unusual Noises
	Hoses		Other: _____

Notes: _____
_____
_____
_____
_____
_____

Operator's Name	Supervisor's Name
_____	_____
Operator's Signature	Supervisor's Signature
_____	_____

PROPANE FORKLIFT INSPECTION CHECKLIST

Date: _____ Shift: _____

Forklift Serial Number: _____

Hour Meter Start: _____ End: _____ Total Hours: _____

	Gas gauge			Hour Meter
	LPG tank and locator pin			Hydraulic Controls
	LPG tank hose			Lights - Head and Tail
	Accelerator			Lights - Warning
	Alarms			Mast
	Battery Connector			Oil Leaks
	Belt			Oil Pressure
	Brakes - Parking			Overhead Guard
	Engine Oil Level			Radiator Level
	Forks			Safety Equipment
	Fuel			Steering
	Gauges			Tires
	Horn			Unusual Noises
	Hoses			Other: _____

Notes: _____
_____
_____
_____
_____
_____
_____

Operator's Name

_____

Operator's Signature

_____

Supervisor's Name

_____

Supervisor's Signature

_____

PROPANE FORKLIFT INSPECTION CHECKLIST

Date: _____ Shift: _____

Forklift Serial Number: _____

Hour Meter Start: _____ End: _____ Total Hours: _____

	Gas gauge		Hour Meter
	LPG tank and locator pin		Hydraulic Controls
	LPG tank hose		Lights - Head and Tail
	Accelerator		Lights - Warning
	Alarms		Mast
	Battery Connector		Oil Leaks
	Belt		Oil Pressure
	Brakes - Parking		Overhead Guard
	Engine Oil Level		Radiator Level
	Forks		Safety Equipment
	Fuel		Steering
	Gauges		Tires
	Horn		Unusual Noises
	Hoses		Other: _____

Notes: _____

_____

_____

_____

_____

_____

Operator's Name

_____

Operator's Signature

_____

Supervisor's Name

_____

Supervisor's Signature

_____

PROPANE FORKLIFT INSPECTION CHECKLIST

Date: _____ Shift: _____

Forklift Serial Number: _____

Hour Meter Start: _____ End: _____ Total Hours: _____

	Gas gauge		Hour Meter
	LPG tank and locator pin		Hydraulic Controls
	LPG tank hose		Lights - Head and Tail
	Accelerator		Lights - Warning
	Alarms		Mast
	Battery Connector		Oil Leaks
	Belt		Oil Pressure
	Brakes - Parking		Overhead Guard
	Engine Oil Level		Radiator Level
	Forks		Safety Equipment
	Fuel		Steering
	Gauges		Tires
	Horn		Unusual Noises
	Hoses		Other: _____

Notes: _____

_____

_____

_____

_____

_____

Operator's Name

_____

Operator's Signature

_____

Supervisor's Name

_____

Supervisor's Signature

_____

PROPANE FORKLIFT INSPECTION CHECKLIST

Date: _____ Shift: _____

Forklift Serial Number: _____

Hour Meter Start: _____ End: _____ Total Hours: _____

	Gas gauge		Hour Meter
	LPG tank and locator pin		Hydraulic Controls
	LPG tank hose		Lights - Head and Tail
	Accelerator		Lights - Warning
	Alarms		Mast
	Battery Connector		Oil Leaks
	Belt		Oil Pressure
	Brakes - Parking		Overhead Guard
	Engine Oil Level		Radiator Level
	Forks		Safety Equipment
	Fuel		Steering
	Gauges		Tires
	Horn		Unusual Noises
	Hoses		Other: _____

Notes: _____

_____

_____

_____

_____

_____

Operator's Name

_____

Operator's Signature

_____

Supervisor's Name

_____

Supervisor's Signature

_____

PROPANE FORKLIFT INSPECTION CHECKLIST

Date: _____ Shift: _____

Forklift Serial Number: _____

Hour Meter Start: _____ End: _____ Total Hours: _____

	Gas gauge		Hour Meter
	LPG tank and locator pin		Hydraulic Controls
	LPG tank hose		Lights - Head and Tail
	Accelerator		Lights - Warning
	Alarms		Mast
	Battery Connector		Oil Leaks
	Belt		Oil Pressure
	Brakes - Parking		Overhead Guard
	Engine Oil Level		Radiator Level
	Forks		Safety Equipment
	Fuel		Steering
	Gauges		Tires
	Horn		Unusual Noises
	Hoses		Other: _____

Notes: _____
_____
_____
_____
_____
_____

Operator's Name

_____

Operator's Signature

_____

Supervisor's Name

_____

Supervisor's Signature

_____

PROPANE FORKLIFT INSPECTION CHECKLIST

Date: _____ Shift: _____

Forklift Serial Number: _____

Hour Meter Start: _____ End: _____ Total Hours: _____

	Gas gauge		Hour Meter
	LPG tank and locator pin		Hydraulic Controls
	LPG tank hose		Lights - Head and Tail
	Accelerator		Lights - Warning
	Alarms		Mast
	Battery Connector		Oil Leaks
	Belt		Oil Pressure
	Brakes - Parking		Overhead Guard
	Engine Oil Level		Radiator Level
	Forks		Safety Equipment
	Fuel		Steering
	Gauges		Tires
	Horn		Unusual Noises
	Hoses		Other: _____

Notes: _____
_____
_____
_____
_____
_____

Operator's Name	Supervisor's Name
_____	_____
Operator's Signature	Supervisor's Signature
_____	_____

PROPANE FORKLIFT INSPECTION CHECKLIST

Date: _____ Shift: _____

Forklift Serial Number: _____

Hour Meter Start: _____ End: _____ Total Hours: _____

	Gas gauge		Hour Meter
	LPG tank and locator pin		Hydraulic Controls
	LPG tank hose		Lights - Head and Tail
	Accelerator		Lights - Warning
	Alarms		Mast
	Battery Connector		Oil Leaks
	Belt		Oil Pressure
	Brakes - Parking		Overhead Guard
	Engine Oil Level		Radiator Level
	Forks		Safety Equipment
	Fuel		Steering
	Gauges		Tires
	Horn		Unusual Noises
	Hoses		Other: _____

Notes: _____
_____
_____
_____
_____
_____

Operator's Name

_____

Operator's Signature

_____

Supervisor's Name

_____

Supervisor's Signature

_____

PROPANE FORKLIFT INSPECTION CHECKLIST

Date: _____ Shift: _____

Forklift Serial Number: _____

Hour Meter Start: _____ End: _____ Total Hours: _____

	Gas gauge		Hour Meter
	LPG tank and locator pin		Hydraulic Controls
	LPG tank hose		Lights - Head and Tail
	Accelerator		Lights - Warning
	Alarms		Mast
	Battery Connector		Oil Leaks
	Belt		Oil Pressure
	Brakes - Parking		Overhead Guard
	Engine Oil Level		Radiator Level
	Forks		Safety Equipment
	Fuel		Steering
	Gauges		Tires
	Horn		Unusual Noises
	Hoses		Other: _____

Notes: _____
_____
_____
_____
_____
_____
_____

Operator's Name

_____

Operator's Signature

_____

Supervisor's Name

_____

Supervisor's Signature

_____

PROPANE FORKLIFT INSPECTION CHECKLIST

Date: _____ Shift: _____

Forklift Serial Number: _____

Hour Meter Start: _____ End: _____ Total Hours: _____

	Gas gauge		Hour Meter
	LPG tank and locator pin		Hydraulic Controls
	LPG tank hose		Lights - Head and Tail
	Accelerator		Lights - Warning
	Alarms		Mast
	Battery Connector		Oil Leaks
	Belt		Oil Pressure
	Brakes - Parking		Overhead Guard
	Engine Oil Level		Radiator Level
	Forks		Safety Equipment
	Fuel		Steering
	Gauges		Tires
	Horn		Unusual Noises
	Hoses		Other: _____

Notes: _____
_____
_____
_____
_____
_____

Operator's Name

_____

Operator's Signature

_____

Supervisor's Name

_____

Supervisor's Signature

_____

PROPANE FORKLIFT INSPECTION CHECKLIST

Date: _____ Shift: _____

Forklift Serial Number: _____

Hour Meter Start: _____ End: _____ Total Hours: _____

	Gas gauge		Hour Meter	
	LPG tank and locator pin		Hydraulic Controls	
	LPG tank hose		Lights - Head and Tail	
	Accelerator		Lights - Warning	
	Alarms		Mast	
	Battery Connector		Oil Leaks	
	Belt		Oil Pressure	
	Brakes - Parking		Overhead Guard	
	Engine Oil Level		Radiator Level	
	Forks		Safety Equipment	
	Fuel		Steering	
	Gauges		Tires	
	Horn		Unusual Noises	
	Hoses		Other: _____	

Notes: _____
_____
_____
_____
_____
_____

Operator's Name

_____

Operator's Signature

_____

Supervisor's Name

_____

Supervisor's Signature

_____

PROPANE FORKLIFT INSPECTION CHECKLIST

Date: _____ Shift: _____

Forklift Serial Number: _____

Hour Meter Start: _____ End: _____ Total Hours: _____

	Gas gauge		Hour Meter
	LPG tank and locator pin		Hydraulic Controls
	LPG tank hose		Lights - Head and Tail
	Accelerator		Lights - Warning
	Alarms		Mast
	Battery Connector		Oil Leaks
	Belt		Oil Pressure
	Brakes - Parking		Overhead Guard
	Engine Oil Level		Radiator Level
	Forks		Safety Equipment
	Fuel		Steering
	Gauges		Tires
	Horn		Unusual Noises
	Hoses		Other: _____

Notes: _____
_____
_____
_____
_____
_____

Operator's Name

_____

Operator's Signature

_____

Supervisor's Name

_____

Supervisor's Signature

_____

PROPANE FORKLIFT INSPECTION CHECKLIST

Date: _____ Shift: _____

Forklift Serial Number: _____

Hour Meter Start: _____ End: _____ Total Hours: _____

	Gas gauge		Hour Meter
	LPG tank and locator pin		Hydraulic Controls
	LPG tank hose		Lights - Head and Tail
	Accelerator		Lights - Warning
	Alarms		Mast
	Battery Connector		Oil Leaks
	Belt		Oil Pressure
	Brakes - Parking		Overhead Guard
	Engine Oil Level		Radiator Level
	Forks		Safety Equipment
	Fuel		Steering
	Gauges		Tires
	Horn		Unusual Noises
	Hoses		Other: _____

Notes: _____
_____
_____
_____
_____
_____
_____

Operator's Name

_____

Operator's Signature

_____

Supervisor's Name

_____

Supervisor's Signature

_____

PROPANE FORKLIFT INSPECTION CHECKLIST

Date: _____ Shift: _____

Forklift Serial Number: _____

Hour Meter Start: _____ End: _____ Total Hours: _____

	Gas gauge		Hour Meter
	LPG tank and locator pin		Hydraulic Controls
	LPG tank hose		Lights - Head and Tail
	Accelerator		Lights - Warning
	Alarms		Mast
	Battery Connector		Oil Leaks
	Belt		Oil Pressure
	Brakes - Parking		Overhead Guard
	Engine Oil Level		Radiator Level
	Forks		Safety Equipment
	Fuel		Steering
	Gauges		Tires
	Horn		Unusual Noises
	Hoses		Other: _____

Notes: _____
_____
_____
_____
_____
_____

Operator's Name

_____

Operator's Signature

_____

Supervisor's Name

_____

Supervisor's Signature

_____

PROPANE FORKLIFT INSPECTION CHECKLIST

Date: _____ Shift: _____

Forklift Serial Number: _____

Hour Meter Start: _____ End: _____ Total Hours: _____

	Gas gauge			Hour Meter
	LPG tank and locator pin			Hydraulic Controls
	LPG tank hose			Lights - Head and Tail
	Accelerator			Lights - Warning
	Alarms			Mast
	Battery Connector			Oil Leaks
	Belt			Oil Pressure
	Brakes - Parking			Overhead Guard
	Engine Oil Level			Radiator Level
	Forks			Safety Equipment
	Fuel			Steering
	Gauges			Tires
	Horn			Unusual Noises
	Hoses			Other: _____

Notes: _____
_____
_____
_____
_____
_____

Operator's Name	Supervisor's Name
_____	_____
Operator's Signature	Supervisor's Signature
_____	_____

PROPANE FORKLIFT INSPECTION CHECKLIST

Date: _____ Shift: _____

Forklift Serial Number: _____

Hour Meter Start: _____ End: _____ Total Hours: _____

	Gas gauge		Hour Meter
	LPG tank and locator pin		Hydraulic Controls
	LPG tank hose		Lights - Head and Tail
	Accelerator		Lights - Warning
	Alarms		Mast
	Battery Connector		Oil Leaks
	Belt		Oil Pressure
	Brakes - Parking		Overhead Guard
	Engine Oil Level		Radiator Level
	Forks		Safety Equipment
	Fuel		Steering
	Gauges		Tires
	Horn		Unusual Noises
	Hoses		Other: _____

Notes: _____

_____

_____

_____

_____

_____

Operator's Name

_____

Operator's Signature

_____

Supervisor's Name

_____

Supervisor's Signature

_____

PROPANE FORKLIFT INSPECTION CHECKLIST

Date: _____ Shift: _____

Forklift Serial Number: _____

Hour Meter Start: _____ End: _____ Total Hours: _____

	Gas gauge		Hour Meter
	LPG tank and locator pin		Hydraulic Controls
	LPG tank hose		Lights - Head and Tail
	Accelerator		Lights - Warning
	Alarms		Mast
	Battery Connector		Oil Leaks
	Belt		Oil Pressure
	Brakes - Parking		Overhead Guard
	Engine Oil Level		Radiator Level
	Forks		Safety Equipment
	Fuel		Steering
	Gauges		Tires
	Horn		Unusual Noises
	Hoses		Other: _____

Notes: _____
_____
_____
_____
_____
_____

Operator's Name

_____

Operator's Signature

_____

Supervisor's Name

_____

Supervisor's Signature

_____

PROPANE FORKLIFT INSPECTION CHECKLIST

Date: _____ Shift: _____

Forklift Serial Number: _____

Hour Meter Start: _____ End: _____ Total Hours: _____

	Gas gauge		Hour Meter
	LPG tank and locator pin		Hydraulic Controls
	LPG tank hose		Lights - Head and Tail
	Accelerator		Lights - Warning
	Alarms		Mast
	Battery Connector		Oil Leaks
	Belt		Oil Pressure
	Brakes - Parking		Overhead Guard
	Engine Oil Level		Radiator Level
	Forks		Safety Equipment
	Fuel		Steering
	Gauges		Tires
	Horn		Unusual Noises
	Hoses		Other: _____

Notes: _____
_____
_____
_____
_____
_____

Operator's Name

_____

Operator's Signature

_____

Supervisor's Name

_____

Supervisor's Signature

_____

PROPANE FORKLIFT INSPECTION CHECKLIST

Date: _____ Shift: _____

Forklift Serial Number: _____

Hour Meter Start: _____ End: _____ Total Hours: _____

	Gas gauge		Hour Meter
	LPG tank and locator pin		Hydraulic Controls
	LPG tank hose		Lights - Head and Tail
	Accelerator		Lights - Warning
	Alarms		Mast
	Battery Connector		Oil Leaks
	Belt		Oil Pressure
	Brakes - Parking		Overhead Guard
	Engine Oil Level		Radiator Level
	Forks		Safety Equipment
	Fuel		Steering
	Gauges		Tires
	Horn		Unusual Noises
	Hoses		Other: _____

Notes: _____
_____
_____
_____
_____
_____

Operator's Name	Supervisor's Name
_____	_____
Operator's Signature	Supervisor's Signature
_____	_____

PROPANE FORKLIFT INSPECTION CHECKLIST

Date: _____ Shift: _____

Forklift Serial Number: _____

Hour Meter Start: _____ End: _____ Total Hours: _____

	Gas gauge		Hour Meter
	LPG tank and locator pin		Hydraulic Controls
	LPG tank hose		Lights - Head and Tail
	Accelerator		Lights - Warning
	Alarms		Mast
	Battery Connector		Oil Leaks
	Belt		Oil Pressure
	Brakes - Parking		Overhead Guard
	Engine Oil Level		Radiator Level
	Forks		Safety Equipment
	Fuel		Steering
	Gauges		Tires
	Horn		Unusual Noises
	Hoses		Other: _____

Notes: _____
_____
_____
_____
_____
_____

Operator's Name
_____

Operator's Signature
_____

Supervisor's Name
_____

Supervisor's Signature
_____

PROPANE FORKLIFT INSPECTION CHECKLIST

Date: _____ Shift: _____

Forklift Serial Number: _____

Hour Meter Start: _____ End: _____ Total Hours: _____

	Gas gauge		Hour Meter
	LPG tank and locator pin		Hydraulic Controls
	LPG tank hose		Lights - Head and Tail
	Accelerator		Lights - Warning
	Alarms		Mast
	Battery Connector		Oil Leaks
	Belt		Oil Pressure
	Brakes - Parking		Overhead Guard
	Engine Oil Level		Radiator Level
	Forks		Safety Equipment
	Fuel		Steering
	Gauges		Tires
	Horn		Unusual Noises
	Hoses		Other: _____

Notes: _____

_____

_____

_____

_____

_____

_____

Operator's Name

_____

Operator's Signature

_____

Supervisor's Name

_____

Supervisor's Signature

_____

PROPANE FORKLIFT INSPECTION CHECKLIST

Date: _____ Shift: _____

Forklift Serial Number: _____

Hour Meter Start: _____ End: _____ Total Hours: _____

	Gas gauge		Hour Meter
	LPG tank and locator pin		Hydraulic Controls
	LPG tank hose		Lights - Head and Tail
	Accelerator		Lights - Warning
	Alarms		Mast
	Battery Connector		Oil Leaks
	Belt		Oil Pressure
	Brakes - Parking		Overhead Guard
	Engine Oil Level		Radiator Level
	Forks		Safety Equipment
	Fuel		Steering
	Gauges		Tires
	Horn		Unusual Noises
	Hoses		Other: _____

Notes: _____
_____
_____
_____
_____
_____
_____

Operator's Name

_____

Operator's Signature

_____

Supervisor's Name

_____

Supervisor's Signature

_____

PROPANE FORKLIFT INSPECTION CHECKLIST

Date: _____ Shift: _____

Forklift Serial Number: _____

Hour Meter Start: _____ End: _____ Total Hours: _____

	Gas gauge		Hour Meter
	LPG tank and locator pin		Hydraulic Controls
	LPG tank hose		Lights - Head and Tail
	Accelerator		Lights - Warning
	Alarms		Mast
	Battery Connector		Oil Leaks
	Belt		Oil Pressure
	Brakes - Parking		Overhead Guard
	Engine Oil Level		Radiator Level
	Forks		Safety Equipment
	Fuel		Steering
	Gauges		Tires
	Horn		Unusual Noises
	Hoses		Other: _____

Notes: _____
_____
_____
_____
_____
_____

Operator's Name

_____

Operator's Signature

_____

Supervisor's Name

_____

Supervisor's Signature

_____

PROPANE FORKLIFT INSPECTION CHECKLIST

Date: _____ Shift: _____

Forklift Serial Number: _____

Hour Meter Start: _____ End: _____ Total Hours: _____

	Gas gauge		Hour Meter
	LPG tank and locator pin		Hydraulic Controls
	LPG tank hose		Lights - Head and Tail
	Accelerator		Lights - Warning
	Alarms		Mast
	Battery Connector		Oil Leaks
	Belt		Oil Pressure
	Brakes - Parking		Overhead Guard
	Engine Oil Level		Radiator Level
	Forks		Safety Equipment
	Fuel		Steering
	Gauges		Tires
	Horn		Unusual Noises
	Hoses		Other: _____

Notes: _____
_____
_____
_____
_____
_____

Operator's Name	Supervisor's Name
_____	_____
Operator's Signature	Supervisor's Signature
_____	_____

PROPANE FORKLIFT INSPECTION CHECKLIST

Date: _____ Shift: _____

Forklift Serial Number: _____

Hour Meter Start: _____ End: _____ Total Hours: _____

	Gas gauge		Hour Meter
	LPG tank and locator pin		Hydraulic Controls
	LPG tank hose		Lights - Head and Tail
	Accelerator		Lights - Warning
	Alarms		Mast
	Battery Connector		Oil Leaks
	Belt		Oil Pressure
	Brakes - Parking		Overhead Guard
	Engine Oil Level		Radiator Level
	Forks		Safety Equipment
	Fuel		Steering
	Gauges		Tires
	Horn		Unusual Noises
	Hoses		Other: _____

Notes: _____

_____

_____

_____

_____

_____

Operator's Name	Supervisor's Name
_____	_____
Operator's Signature	Supervisor's Signature
_____	_____

PROPANE FORKLIFT INSPECTION CHECKLIST

Date: _____ Shift: _____

Forklift Serial Number: _____

Hour Meter Start: _____ End: _____ Total Hours: _____

	Gas gauge		Hour Meter
	LPG tank and locator pin		Hydraulic Controls
	LPG tank hose		Lights - Head and Tail
	Accelerator		Lights - Warning
	Alarms		Mast
	Battery Connector		Oil Leaks
	Belt		Oil Pressure
	Brakes - Parking		Overhead Guard
	Engine Oil Level		Radiator Level
	Forks		Safety Equipment
	Fuel		Steering
	Gauges		Tires
	Horn		Unusual Noises
	Hoses		Other: _____

Notes: _____
_____
_____
_____
_____
_____

Operator's Name
_____

Operator's Signature
_____

Supervisor's Name
_____

Supervisor's Signature
_____

PROPANE FORKLIFT INSPECTION CHECKLIST

Date: _____ Shift: _____

Forklift Serial Number: _____

Hour Meter Start: _____ End: _____ Total Hours: _____

	Gas gauge			Hour Meter
	LPG tank and locator pin			Hydraulic Controls
	LPG tank hose			Lights - Head and Tail
	Accelerator			Lights - Warning
	Alarms			Mast
	Battery Connector			Oil Leaks
	Belt			Oil Pressure
	Brakes - Parking			Overhead Guard
	Engine Oil Level			Radiator Level
	Forks			Safety Equipment
	Fuel			Steering
	Gauges			Tires
	Horn			Unusual Noises
	Hoses			Other: _____

Notes: _____
_____
_____
_____
_____
_____

Operator's Name

_____

Operator's Signature

_____

Supervisor's Name

_____

Supervisor's Signature

_____

PROPANE FORKLIFT INSPECTION CHECKLIST

Date: _____ Shift: _____

Forklift Serial Number: _____

Hour Meter Start: _____ End: _____ Total Hours: _____

	Gas gauge		Hour Meter
	LPG tank and locator pin		Hydraulic Controls
	LPG tank hose		Lights - Head and Tail
	Accelerator		Lights - Warning
	Alarms		Mast
	Battery Connector		Oil Leaks
	Belt		Oil Pressure
	Brakes - Parking		Overhead Guard
	Engine Oil Level		Radiator Level
	Forks		Safety Equipment
	Fuel		Steering
	Gauges		Tires
	Horn		Unusual Noises
	Hoses		Other: _____

Notes: _____
_____
_____
_____
_____
_____

Operator's Name	Supervisor's Name
_____	_____
Operator's Signature	Supervisor's Signature
_____	_____

PROPANE FORKLIFT INSPECTION CHECKLIST

Date: _____ Shift: _____

Forklift Serial Number: _____

Hour Meter Start: _____ End: _____ Total Hours: _____

	Gas gauge		Hour Meter
	LPG tank and locator pin		Hydraulic Controls
	LPG tank hose		Lights - Head and Tail
	Accelerator		Lights - Warning
	Alarms		Mast
	Battery Connector		Oil Leaks
	Belt		Oil Pressure
	Brakes - Parking		Overhead Guard
	Engine Oil Level		Radiator Level
	Forks		Safety Equipment
	Fuel		Steering
	Gauges		Tires
	Horn		Unusual Noises
	Hoses		Other: _____

Notes: _____
_____
_____
_____
_____
_____

Operator's Name	Supervisor's Name
_____	_____
Operator's Signature	Supervisor's Signature
_____	_____

PROPANE FORKLIFT INSPECTION CHECKLIST

Date: _____ Shift: _____

Forklift Serial Number: _____

Hour Meter Start: _____ End: _____ Total Hours: _____

	Gas gauge		Hour Meter
	LPG tank and locator pin		Hydraulic Controls
	LPG tank hose		Lights - Head and Tail
	Accelerator		Lights - Warning
	Alarms		Mast
	Battery Connector		Oil Leaks
	Belt		Oil Pressure
	Brakes - Parking		Overhead Guard
	Engine Oil Level		Radiator Level
	Forks		Safety Equipment
	Fuel		Steering
	Gauges		Tires
	Horn		Unusual Noises
	Hoses		Other: _____

Notes: _____

_____

_____

_____

_____

_____

Operator's Name	Supervisor's Name
_____	_____
Operator's Signature	Supervisor's Signature
_____	_____

PROPANE FORKLIFT INSPECTION CHECKLIST

Date: _____ Shift: _____

Forklift Serial Number: _____

Hour Meter Start: _____ End: _____ Total Hours: _____

	Gas gauge		Hour Meter
	LPG tank and locator pin		Hydraulic Controls
	LPG tank hose		Lights - Head and Tail
	Accelerator		Lights - Warning
	Alarms		Mast
	Battery Connector		Oil Leaks
	Belt		Oil Pressure
	Brakes - Parking		Overhead Guard
	Engine Oil Level		Radiator Level
	Forks		Safety Equipment
	Fuel		Steering
	Gauges		Tires
	Horn		Unusual Noises
	Hoses		Other: _____

Notes: _____
_____
_____
_____
_____
_____
_____

Operator's Name	Supervisor's Name
_____	_____
Operator's Signature	Supervisor's Signature
_____	_____

PROPANE FORKLIFT INSPECTION CHECKLIST

Date: _____ Shift: _____

Forklift Serial Number: _____

Hour Meter Start: _____ End: _____ Total Hours: _____

Gas gauge	Hour Meter
LPG tank and locator pin	Hydraulic Controls
LPG tank hose	Lights - Head and Tail
Accelerator	Lights - Warning
Alarms	Mast
Battery Connector	Oil Leaks
Belt	Oil Pressure
Brakes - Parking	Overhead Guard
Engine Oil Level	Radiator Level
Forks	Safety Equipment
Fuel	Steering
Gauges	Tires
Horn	Unusual Noises
Hoses	Other: _____

Notes: _____
_____
_____
_____
_____
_____

Operator's Name	Supervisor's Name
_____	_____
Operator's Signature	Supervisor's Signature
_____	_____

PROPANE FORKLIFT INSPECTION CHECKLIST

Date: _____ Shift: _____

Forklift Serial Number: _____

Hour Meter Start: _____ End: _____ Total Hours: _____

	Gas gauge		Hour Meter
	LPG tank and locator pin		Hydraulic Controls
	LPG tank hose		Lights - Head and Tail
	Accelerator		Lights - Warning
	Alarms		Mast
	Battery Connector		Oil Leaks
	Belt		Oil Pressure
	Brakes - Parking		Overhead Guard
	Engine Oil Level		Radiator Level
	Forks		Safety Equipment
	Fuel		Steering
	Gauges		Tires
	Horn		Unusual Noises
	Hoses		Other: _____

Notes: _____
_____
_____
_____
_____
_____

Operator's Name

_____

Operator's Signature

_____

Supervisor's Name

_____

Supervisor's Signature

_____

PROPANE FORKLIFT INSPECTION CHECKLIST

Date: _____ Shift: _____

Forklift Serial Number: _____

Hour Meter Start: _____ End: _____ Total Hours: _____

	Gas gauge		Hour Meter
	LPG tank and locator pin		Hydraulic Controls
	LPG tank hose		Lights - Head and Tail
	Accelerator		Lights - Warning
	Alarms		Mast
	Battery Connector		Oil Leaks
	Belt		Oil Pressure
	Brakes - Parking		Overhead Guard
	Engine Oil Level		Radiator Level
	Forks		Safety Equipment
	Fuel		Steering
	Gauges		Tires
	Horn		Unusual Noises
	Hoses		Other: _____

Notes: _____
_____
_____
_____
_____
_____

Operator's Name	Supervisor's Name
_____	_____
Operator's Signature	Supervisor's Signature
_____	_____

Made in the USA
Las Vegas, NV
04 February 2025

17551355R00203